DIVINE INTERVENTION

The Story of the Luciferian Conspiracy and God's Solutions

DIVINE INTERVENTION

The Story of the Luciferian Conspiracy
and God's Solutions

Received by
Adriene Wentworth

Library of Congress Catalog Card Number: 97-91957

ISBN 0 - 9654365 - 0 - 0

Published by:
CHRISTA RESOURCES
P.O. Box 696
Prior Lake, MN 55372

Printed in the United States of America

To Tara, whose heart was touched by
the cries for help and responded
by giving and giving and giving.

CONTENTS

ACKNOWLEDGMENTS

This book would never have been created without the support, love and dedication of Leela Gram and Tara Tindall. These two angels have stood by me through it all. They've cared for my children who are now just as much their children, giving me the much needed time and space to do whatever I needed to do whenever I needed to do it. They have spent endless hours helping me edit and convert the verbal messages I received from Spirit into smooth flowing written text. Leela and Tara, may God fill you with Divine Grace and bless you many times for all you've sacrificed to support me. Thank you for walking this path with me, it hasn't always been easy, yet your sincere friendship and commitment has cleared the way many times.

Adriene's Foreword

The first time I saw Lucifer he was standing in front of a spaceship leading people inside. He saw me watching and acknowledged my presence with a cold, determined glare. In that brief moment he let me know that he was going to continue doing what he was doing, and as I met his glare I let him know that I was going to do whatever I could to stop him. I awoke from this dream vision in terror. My mind was racing. Why did I think I could stop Lucifer, and what was he doing anyway? It took me many years to understand the significance of this dream experience.

I feel it is important to share with you some of my background and how I came to channel this book. I began my spiritual journey at the age of twenty-two. I constantly had experiences with the psychic realms that I didn't really understand. Those experiences motivated me to seek out spiritual teachers and knowledge to help me cope and understand what was happening to me. I feel very blessed to have had the guidance that led me to two Himalayan Masters who shared their knowledge and skills with me. I traveled to India three times to study with these Himalayan Masters and completed intensive training in Jnana Yoga (the path of knowledge and intellect), Bhakti Yoga (the path of love and devotion), Raja Yoga (the path of discipline and meditation), and Kundalini Yoga (the path of primal force). These Himalayan Masters kept close watch over my spiritual process. Together, they guided me to God

Consciousness and stayed with me until I could comfortably reach this Consciousness on my own.

During this period I had numerous blissful spiritual experiences as my kundalini energy rose higher and higher, and yet these experiences were also sometimes mixed with frightening encounters with astral entities and powerful negative forces. This disturbed me so deeply that I began searching for what was causing this interference and what could be done to prevent it. The spiritual community wasn't much help. One spiritual teacher simply told me that astral beings didn't exist and that nothing impure could happen in a pure mind. Basically, I was warned not to delve into these matters. I continued to pray for guidance and eventually was led to a spiritual Master who taught me how to empower mantras for protection, but even though this helped, the vulnerabilities were still there. I began an extensive study of our energetic bodies. I studied and apprenticed with numerous teachers and healers and practiced everything I learned from them, and yet the answers were not there. A strong spiritual force kept pushing me to continue my quest for Truth.

Throughout my journey, Lord Jesus has been my trusted companion and guiding force, and Archangel Michael has kept a constant watch over my spiritual development and experiences. Jesus and Archangel Michael often took me to other dimensions to meet with other Beings of Light who looked like Ancient Ones and Native Americans for training and to answer my questions. With their guidance I began to uncover, one by one, all of the dark force interferences in our energy bodies and developed techniques to remove them. I was then gifted with the Christa Energy which protects against these forces once the interferences and vulnerabilities are removed.

I never intended to become a channeler of information, for in the yogic traditions one is taught to ignore the psychic abilities that naturally occur as one develops spiritually and keep all energies focused on achieving the highest goal of yoga, which is to merge the individual self with the Universal Self. I did not begin channeling until I accomplished this goal and began to receive messages from the beautiful Beings of Light who I had become attuned to during my spiritual journey.

I became familiar with the Ancient Ones who had formed a Council in the earliest of times to rescue lost souls. This Ancient Council, now referred to as the Ancient Spiritual Hierarchy, consists of the Father and Mother Aspects of God, Archangel Michael, Ashtar, Sananda (the High Self aspect of Jesus) and Mother Mary. These Superbeings began training me to be their spokesperson and deliver their messages to the people of the Earth. The vibrations of the Ancient Ones that I channel are extremely powerful and have not been stepped-down. Their messages are to the point and are not softened for comfort. Each channel interprets information according to their knowledge, experience and personality. Because of my extensive training in yoga and meditation, I have built a solid bridge through the dimensions to the Source and can receive these powerful energies. I was also given experiences to create an opening for the kind of information I receive.

DIVINE INTERVENTION

I was asked to channel this story to help you become aware of what is going on within our energy bodies and the planet we inhabit. I believe this information was given in a story form to help you absorb the difficult subject matter without shutting down with fear and resistance. This story is empowered with strong vibrations to enable the information to bypass your implants and other dark force interferences. It will trigger you to remember your own connection to the Source of God and how to call upon that connection now to lift you out of the darkness, so that you can again know Truth. You will also remember many painful experiences that you have deeply buried or have been programmed to forget.

During the course of my healing experience I have learned that many people remain powerless because they do not know that their power has been taken. Also because of so many lifetimes of abusing power and being abused by power, many choose to stay asleep and unaware rather than take responsibility for their own destinies. We are often easy victims to the forces that prey on our energies. God can only help us if we choose to help ourselves. This story is offered to those who are crying out for help as they become aware of the battles going on within them and their host planet, Mother Earth. It takes courage to expand the scope of your vision and strong determination to break through all of the illusions and barriers that are so ingrained into our existence.

There are many levels of information presented in this story. If you read it several times you will notice different vibrational shifts taking place within you and experience higher understandings. This story gently guides the way, winding around all of your set belief systems, constantly reassuring you to go further and explore more. The spiritual journey has always been the experience of emerging from the Source of God, falling into darkness and illusion because of naiveté and lack of wisdom, creating experiences for learning and then with full knowledge, finding the way back to the Source. Now, because of the numerous interferences, many are not able to free themselves and find their way Home. When things get too out of balance God intervenes. The Bhagavad Gita (4.7-8), reminds us of this Divine Intervention: "Whenever dharma declines and the purpose of life is forgotten, (the Divine) manifests itself on earth ... to protect the good, to destroy evil and to reestablish dharma[1]."

Yours in service to the One,
Adriene K. Wentworth
May 1997

---

[1]**dharma** [Skt. darmah, law.] **1.** The ultimate law of all things in Hinduism and Buddhism. **2.** Individual right conduct in conformity to dharma. Webster's II, New Riverside University Dictionary.

SECTION I

DIVINE INTERVENTION

The Story of the Luciferian Conspiracy
and God's Solutions

Introduction

The ANCIENT HIERARCHY speaks:

We have joined our consciousness to speak to you throughout these channelings. At times we will individualize ourselves and speak to you as separate entities. We are ancient vibrations of the Beings you know as the Mother and Father aspects of God, Archangel Michael, Ashtar, Sananda (the High Self aspect of Jesus) and Mother Mary.

We are here today to begin explaining how important it is for you, the people of the Earth, to understand the effects that other beings have on you and how you are being influenced in your thinking. It is very important to understand that you are all susceptible. If you understand what is happening to you, you can seek out the knowledge to be safe and to prevent interference. But without the wisdom of knowing what is interfering with you, you become a victim, and victimization is something that needs to end for the people of the Earth. Many are victims and many are being influenced without their agreement.

One of the most obvious interferences are cordings. You have numerous cordings at many levels of your existence. These cordings interfere with your ability to find your own way, to see clearly your own chosen path. Through these cordings the belief systems and the desires of others influence you to stay where the persons corded to you would like you to stay. They pull on you and subtly change the energy forms within you. The positive and good

3

thought forms you are so sincerely trying to create are changed by this negative charge in the body. The negative energy comes in through the cording and the positive energy is dissipated. It feels as if you are getting nowhere in your spirituality or in creating balance and happiness in your life.

These cordings are something that you need to be aware of. You have been corded so often you no longer know what is at the core of your being. You are wrapped in numerous cordings which are tight webbings of energy that hold you in place. These cordings need to be severed and cut and the negatively charged energy moved out of your bodies. This will free your energy to flow with the Oneness of the Source of All.

You must reconnect and attune to God's Energy which will help you manifest what you need to move your life forward. You have learned to stress out your bodies and are not drawing on God's Energy, which flows always and is there for everyone. It is always there flowing. You can connect up to God's Energy anytime you choose. It does not take much practice. It takes willingness and openness to allow God's Energy to flow within you. Open your minds and your hearts to understand this concept. It is possible to attune to God's Energy and again create with God. It is time for you to remember how to manifest. It is time to demonstrate your power of faith and belief in the Oneness and Goodness of the Source. To be able to manifest one must be clear of all interference. This is so critically important.

We will speak to you about the dark forces. This is a subject which is distorted in so many ways on your Earth, and you now need to clearly see the

4

Introduction

Truth. There are beings on the Earth now who have been created by men. They have been created by men to manipulate, to harm and to hoard energy as well as material things. These beings have been sustained by much negativity of thinking throughout the ages. These beings have become so strong in nature that they have created brotherhoods of their own, which we call the dark brotherhoods. These brotherhoods exist now in many dimensions. They have linked up their energy sources to become quite vast in nature and are now a powerful impediment to the people of the Earth, as well as other beings on other planets and in other time dimensions.

The beings that make up the dark brotherhoods have been created by the participation of the people on your planet and also by the participation of beings on other planets. The original source of their existence came from the minds of men. Most people tend to think that if one does not think about dark force beings they will not exist. They do exist. Each one of you must understand they do exist, for they have already been created and must be dealt with because they are interfering with you and your loved ones. These energies of darkness do not pick and choose who they attack and prey on. They do not discern between the young or old, spiritually evolved or completely sound asleep. These energies prey on all they can enter, and their ways of entering are many. If you are not cleared of all of their hook-ins they will enter and control your being, your destinies and your happiness, and this is not to be allowed. These forces have become so powerful that God has asked a group of Light Beings to come to Earth and clear the interferences that these dark ones are creating.

Your Earth Mother is suffering greatly from the hold of these dark energies. She wants them out. They are poison to her system. They hurt her. They are cruel. They care not for her nurturance, her beauty or her love. They destroy all they come in contact with, and they are now in contact with many beings on the Earth. They are now intertwined and intermingled with many people on the Earth who have allowed them entrance, most unknowingly. Most are victims in a sense, for unknowingly they have opened themselves to these dark forces by their own negative thinking and by their desire for power, power over others and power over the universe and the way it flows and creates. Many have desired to take charge and rule over the Earth with a tight reign. The Earth was not meant to be leashed in this way. The Earth is prepared to unleash now and is asking for assistance.

The EARTH MOTHER speaks:

My pain is great. I am swollen with pain. I cannot hold this pain much longer, my children. It is festering within. You must quit trying to prevent me from releasing my pain. Please cooperate now with me and the Beings of Light who are here to help us and with the Brotherhoods of Light who are trying to assist from other dimensions. We are all working together and we are asking you to wake up and consciously see how you are participating. Where are you aligned? Are you aligned with me and the Light, or are you aligned with the dark forces? If you have chosen the dark forces, you will be shucked off my surface and spewed out into the atmosphere. There will be no one there to rescue you.

The call for you to awaken and be responsible for your creations, to treat others fairly and equally and to share in the abundance and the goodness that is there for one and all, has been going out for some time. This call has been ignored. You have allowed the dark forces to influence you. They have convinced you that they are masters of creation and their way is the way of greatness. You have become their pawns and your energy is being taken from you. It is being sucked from the very core of your being each moment you cooperate with them.

It is now time for action. I will be taking action. I will show you that I am a powerful force. I have God-given power. I have allowed much abuse. I am no longer going to allow it, for now my very existence is threatened. I must transform and become lighter. Only those who are willing to transform and become lighter along with me will be allowed to stay on my surface.

Please listen now, my children. I plead with you to listen and allow the vibration of what is being said to penetrate your darkness. You all have the opportunity now to open and become Light and align with the Source of All, your Creator. This is your Earth Mother speaking. I have consciousness and I can communicate to those who are attuned to me. I will tell you of my intended actions.

ASHTAR speaks:

There is a grand illusion on your planet that is keeping you separate from parts of yourself. Stretch your minds and allow the energies to come through to help you understand and remember who you are.

There are many conspiracies on your planet and each time one is uncovered it is like peeling away a veil and you can see more clearly. So many of you are here to assist humanity and the Earth and yet very strong negative programming is keeping you from waking up and coming forward with the unique knowledge and wisdom you carry within.

You and your planet are so polluted. It hurts us to see the levels of pollution in your physical vehicles. It is time to allow the purification that will make each one of you feel good again. We understand why you have become frustrated and despondent as you battle the heavy levels of energy you must deal with every day of your earthly existence. It is time to clear these heavy energies from you and the Earth. The healing and transformational energies that we are sending to you and your Earth Mother to help you lighten up are being interfered with in many different ways. There are disruptive frequencies that are being sent through very large satellite dishes that are keeping you ill. Your planet is being preyed on by many different groups of extraterrestrials who have been depleting your soul essence and the natural resources of your Earth. We watch your minds try to cope with this difficult information. Many of you do not want to know, "Let's just turn the TV back on and watch something that will pacify us." If you do not know what is happening how will you know what to do when God now steps in to help?

All of you have spiritual guides who have been assigned to help you with your spiritual growth process. Ask your guides to be present while you read this book to help you assimilate the information presented. Ask them to show you where you are blocked and not in alignment with God's Energy.

ARCHANGEL MICHAEL speaks:

I am a force field. Attune to my energy and raise your energy to connect with me. I can expand my energy as far as I choose to, I can keep going further and further. I want to teach you how to expand as I expand. Visualize me as a disk above you, intricate in nature with many different dimensions, an energy that fills as much space as is needed. I want you to learn to become space like this so you can assist me. I am a protector. I will teach those who are willing to work with my energy how to shelter others.

There are many who are seeking assistance and are never going to be drawn to the right place at the right time. They are going to need a shelter energy to help absorb the impact of what is to come. Think of it as applying insulation to make an impact less harsh, like a giant air bag. This is important and needed, for we are getting ready to draw your Earth out of the darkness she is stuck in. We cannot wait much longer. At this time we are stabilizing and holding the Earth in place until more of you are awake and activated.

Many of you have forgotten how powerful your energies are. You have forgotten how you can positively affect other people. You have limited yourselves. You have forgotten that you used to know how to fly through the air. It was not a challenge for you. You just flew through the air. Yes, you did this. You looked at a tree and you said, "That tree is so lovely, I am going to experience what it feels like to be that tree." And you changed your form and you became a tree. Now you're all thinking, "But that was very long ago." It has been so long that you have forgotten how to use your full potential. You have forgotten how joyful it is to be in your power. When you are in your power and you are aligned with God, the joy is exquisite. Are you happy with your life at this time? Do you know any people who are happy and fulfilled and content with their lives?

There is a lot of information circulating around your Earth plane about the coming changes. It is important for you to understand and accept why these Earth changes must occur and rally yourself to participate. We will explain everything to you and it will be a stretch for your mind. We can sense you thinking, "Why do people need to be sheltered? What is the impact that needs cushioning? What is going on?"

God would like to deliver a message to you. You must be willing to open to it. You're probably thinking, "Oh, God, no! Archangel Michael, that's good enough — but God? We're not ready for God, are we?"

Introduction

Get ready for God! He wants you to connect with His Energy so badly, and you are feeling, "No, we are working our way up to God." God says, "Would you just let Me in? I am knocking at your door."

GOD speaks:

Long ago . . . long ago, when you emerged out of My Essence there were great celebrations with trumpets blaring. It was the most spectacular light show you could possibly imagine. You emerged with so much enthusiasm as you made your grand entrance. It was as if you were saying, "I am alive! I am born! Oh, thank-you, thank-you!" We celebrated and danced with joy. And after the celebration you asked, "What am I supposed to do now that I am here? Celebrating is fun, but what else can I do?"

I answered, "Experience, create, go out and explore and then come back and tell Me all of your stories. We will always be together as I will be watching over your every move. Whatever you experience I also will experience for we are connected. You are a Ray that burst out of Me and everything you experience I will feel. My nature is to create and experience. So go out, go out and do whatever you want!"

I did not know you would move away from Me and not find your way back. Many of you are confused and think, "God knows exactly what is going to happen. It has already been written." It has not. Would I write a plan for a world full of pain and misery, and then have to feel all that pain Myself? Why would I put that punishment upon Myself when everything you feel I feel?

When you pick a flower and are moved by its beauty, I am also moved. When your heart is broken and you are crying, I feel your pain and want to comfort you and say, "Come back, come back to where it is safe, come back to where it is loving."

I never wanted you to go so far away from Me. You have been fooled. You have been tricked. It is not your fault. We are in this together. I am just as responsible for what has happened as you are. I am trying to help you, but you have to open and listen to what is preventing you from being able to come back to Me. You have been gone so long, you don't think you have a Home anymore. You live on the Earth plane, but do you feel safe? Do you feel like Earth is your home? What is it that you think of as home? Isn't home a place where you can go and the ideal is, "I am home. I can be myself. I can kick my shoes off. I can relax because I am accepted here." This is what home is supposed to be like. Do you ever feel unconditionally loved? That is what I am offering you, unconditional love. Come Home, come Home. You pray to Me, "Why aren't You taking care of me? I'm so afraid. I'm so confused."

You must now open to the understanding of what is going on so that I can help you. I have so much power and that power belongs to you. It is your birthright. I want you to again align with My Energy so you are safe, so you are protected, so you can create the realities that you need.

Do you know that I have had to create realities that you can accept because so many are out of alignment? I have had to do it this way to bring the masses up so they can touch Me again. Throughout history My messengers have had to deliver messages that could be accepted at the time. "Okay, I will create this reality because they can accept this reality, but they cannot really accept the Truth yet." This is how you are taken through stages. Now it is time to reveal to you more Truth.

The Truth is you are being manipulated and interfered with. There is much dark energy within you preventing you from reaching Me. You are holding out your outstretched arms and you are saying, "Father, why can't I reach You? I do want to." I can help you but you will have to claim back your own personal power and be willing to work with Me. It is a cooperative effort between us. My Plan to help you keeps changing. It has to be adjusted according to your readiness. Time is running out for you to reconnect with My Light.

You are expending too much of your energy focusing on material gain. How long will your house stand when the Earth begins to shake? Your Earth Mother cries out to Me constantly, "Why are You allowing this? When are You going to step in and change this?" And I say, "Mother, be patient. I know you are hurting. Be patient, because if we have opportunity to save more souls then we must hang in there a little longer." When we are at the point when we must move forward, I will stop the stabilization and begin the activation. When I begin the activation it will feel like nothing you have ever experienced before. Your physical reality will change and if you are not aligned with My Energy you will not know how to function. It is so important that you come into alignment with Me now and then help others to do so.

AFFIRMATIONS

I choose to connect up to God's Energy.

I willingly open and allow God's Energy to flow within me.

I open my mind and my heart to God. I remember that I have the ability to attune to God's Energy and to again create with God.

I am aligned with God's Light and am willing to assist the Earth Mother with her clearing and healing.

I take responsibility for what I create. I treat others fairly and equally. I share in the abundance and goodness that is here for one and all.

I now take action. I am willing to transform and become lighter along with Mother Earth.

As I awaken to my true nature I experience incredible joy and this vibration assists everyone I interact with.

I ask my spiritual guides to show me where I am blocked and not in alignment with God's Energy.

I release all limitations and remember how powerful my energies are and how I can positively affect other people. When I hold the high vibrations of peacefulness, centeredness, love and joy, everyone who walks into my presence will benefit.

AFFIRMATIONS

I allow God to help me find my way Home by opening to His Energy and by listening to what has been preventing my return.

God's power belongs to me, it is my birthright. As I align with God's Energy, I am protected and safe.

I reclaim my personal power.

I am willing to work cooperatively with God to release all dark energies and reconnect to His Light.

ONE

FROM FREEDOM TO BONDAGE

Long ago in the Land of Pan, all were happy, all were joyous, all were able to leap in and out of forms with just a thought. "What would it feel like to swim like a dolphin?" With just a thought, fish-like fins and gills would form and you would leap into crystal-clear blue sparkling water and lightness and laughter would prevail. This is still possible, my children. Why have you forgotten your God-given power to create? Why have you decided that life needs to be heavy, that life needs to be a struggle, when you have been given the gift of changing form? You have the ability to change into whatever you desire. The grossness of matter is not an impediment if one is aligned with the Light. Much has been said about these earlier times. Much has been written about the Land of Pan, but the fall needs to be understood. For it is here, my darling children, that the story of darkness begins.

When you were created you were created in love. You were created with joy. This was all you knew, love and joy. The Source of All, the Source of Light, the Source of Truth, which you call God, created you. God

17

created you by merging with His own Energy. He gave you birth through His love of Self, not of another, for there was no other, just One, just Self. He birthed Himself through Himself into many glorious dazzling Rays of Light, each just varying enough from the other to create the most magnificent streams of pulsating vibrations. You are these beautiful Rays of Light, my children. The Source of All merged His Energy inward until He could hold the tension no longer. Then with a burst of ecstasy, so delicious, He released this tension that sent out Rays of His Energy in all directions. Those Rays are you, my children. The joy and pleasure your God felt by creating you stimulated Him to keep creating. It was just energy playing with energy, Light playing with Light.

You were created with joy. You were created with love, with intense ecstatic pleasure, and then you were allowed to experience. You were separate yet you were attached to the Source in a most wondrous way. You could merge into the Source as deep as you wanted to go, and then you could go flying, furling out, excitedly searching places that were unknown to you. Yet you were very secure, understanding you could go back to the Source whenever you desired. It was a wonderful secure feeling. You were always connected to the Source of All. You explored many realms and many dimensions and took joy in bringing back your experiences to share with each other. You would share among yourselves and then take your experiences back to the Source. The Source would shed Light on your discoveries and you would become One again.

What happened then, my children? Why did you lose your connection? Did God Himself, the wonderful Source of Light and Love, throw you down to Earth? No, that is not the way it happened. We are here to tell you the Truth. That is not the way it happened. The Source of All was very content and happy watching His creations learn, explore and revel in His Light. He enjoyed it. It was completely satisfying.

One day, and day has no meaning here but to help you understand in a story form, one day there was darkness. This darkness appeared to be Light. It appeared to be similar to the God-Source. It appeared to be powerful. It appeared to be loving, but it was very cunning. This darkness was a reflection of the Source of All, created in opposition to Its Goodness. This darkness came about in a most natural way, for as more and more was created from the Source of All, reflections started to appear around the Light.

These reflections were like mirror images which seemed similar to the Light creations, yet they held no Truth within them. These reflections were intended to guide you, the Rays of Light, and help you stay true to your Light.

But this is not what happened. As we look around the Earth plane today we see how few have learned from their reflections. A reflection is not to be taken in and allowed to flow and control the Light. God Himself had no idea what would come about when the reflections began to take form. He had no idea of the havoc that would be caused or the pain and suffering that would come about when the Rays of Light began to explore these reflections and add energy to them until they became a viable living force -- a viable living force that began to grow and control the Beings of Light who were only exploring.

This darkness began to take a strong hold within these Rays. As these Rays would attempt to merge back into the One, the Source of All, this darkness would hold them tight. There was much confusion. Fear was felt for the first time, for it had always been so easy, so natural to flow back into the One. It was just understood. It was the natural way of existing, flowing back, coming out, flowing back, coming out. There was never any resistance. Now for the first time they met resistance. It was as if ropes were tied to their feet. As they tried to ascend back to the Source they were pulled back down to the lower planes, the planes they had only gone to explore. They had no intention of staying in these lower planes.

The Rays of Light struggled to release themselves from the tight grips the negative energies had on them and in their panic and confusion they let go of their God connection. This was their mistake. When they let go of their connection, the darkness pulled them down and into the realms of the unconscious, to the velvet blackness where no Light existed.

These now lost Rays, lost souls, began to lament. They cried out, "Oh Father, God of All, oh Mother of Creation, why have You abandoned us? What happened? We trusted You. Why didn't You save us? Why did You let us go? Now what will we do? We are frightened. We are in terror. This darkness is suffocating us. We can see no way out. We are so confused. We don't know what to do. We are dying. The memory of You is fading so fast. The memory of Your Light, the memory of the joy, the ecstatic joy we experienced, is fading. All we feel now is heaviness, much, much heaviness. We feel so burdened now."

There was a time, my children, when your fate could have been changed. You did not trust that the Source of All had the power to pull you up and release you from this darkness. As children who played too adventuresome and got into trouble, you did not trust that your Father of All, your Mother of Creation, could have saved you. You did not see that Their power was ready and waiting to pull you back up, to bring you back into the Source where all is Light, all is Goodness. But you, my children, you let go. You did not even cry out. You just let go and began struggling and struggling with this darkness yourself. All you needed to do was allow your Mother, your Father, to pull you out, to bring you back to safety, to clean you off and love you.

You were always loved. You were never abandoned. You were never judged for your folly, for you were young in spirit and you were only exploring. This is a gift that the Source had given to you. "My children, go out as far and as long as you want and know that I am here. I am here always. We are connected. You are always safe, for I am here, we are connected," is what He told you.

Why is it that you no longer believe that the Source of Goodness is there for you? So much has transpired, so much pain and darkness. My children, you need to connect up again. You have to let go of this darkness and make an effort to connect up again. It is not difficult nor hard to do. This same darkness, these same dark forces that held you tight and fooled you into thinking you were trapped and that your God was not powerful enough to save you, are still holding you back from feeling your connection, from finding it and making it firm.

These forces prey on your vulnerabilities, your doubts, your fears. This is how they enter. It is so easy. You have made it so easy for them. There is so much room for them to enter. Your energy bodies are full of holes. You are corded to other beings who are corded to this darkness. It just flows from one to the other, like water through a faucet. There is no way of turning it off unless you cut these cords, pull them out at their very roots and take back your power. You must take back your power and align yourself again with the God of All, the God of Goodness, the God of Light.

We have watched many of you struggle with these concepts. We have seen the struggles in your minds and we have seen behind the struggles to the influence of the dark forces, the influences holding you stuck in your belief systems. "There is no such thing as dark beings. There is no such thing," you tell yourself. This is not true. These beings exist. You gave them form yourselves by giving your reflections energy. You breathed life into them and they began to multiply within themselves. It is the process of manifestation. It is creation creating itself. It was a misuse of the wonderful power that was given to you by the God of All, the God of Oneness, the God of Goodness. He gave you the power to create, to manifest. He gave you the reflection to guide you in what you manifested and created, but your spirits were young and adventuresome and you decided to play in ways that were not in alignment with the Source. Again, there was no judgment, for the God of All, the God of Goodness, understood that you were just experiencing and exploring as children do and it was allowed, because the God of Oneness knew He could draw you back to safety whenever you were ready to come back. When you had had enough of your play He could draw you back.

But you, my children, felt guilt for the first time. You felt unworthy of being drawn back because of what you had done, for you knew you dabbled where you shouldn't have. You played with energy and created forms that were not in alignment with the Light and you felt unworthy.

You felt ashamed. When these forms became so real and alive and began to pull on you and hold you, instead of calling out like children to your very loving parents, who would have been there in an instant, you were ashamed and you struggled within yourselves. You attempted to hide your feelings from God thinking, "I hope I can release myself and find my way back Home and no one will need to know what I have done. I am so ashamed." The God of All knew what you were doing and did not judge you and condemn you to a dark place. He allowed you to choose your destiny. He allowed you to choose.

You must now let go of any shame and any guilt that you are holding from these early times of your existence. We hear your thoughts, "Why was I so stupid? If I was a Being of Light, why was I so stupid? Why did I get involved with this?" My children, you were young spirits. You knew only Love and Light. You were only exploring. God gave you a reflection to look at, to learn from, to keep you on track with what you created. This reflection showed you the power of creation. It showed you what could be created if you misused this power. The reflection presented your every thought like images in a mirror. You found these images to be so interesting and enticing that you were drawn to add your energy and manifesting power to them. When these images came to life they were so seductive in nature that you couldn't resist playing with them. This is how you became entrapped in these reflections.

AFFIRMATIONS

I remember my God-given power to create.

I was created in love and joy. The Source of All, the Source of Light and Truth, created me. I am a beautiful Ray of God's Light.

I know the Source of Goodness is there for me. Once I let go of all dark interference and connect back up to God's Light, my Father of All, my Mother of Creation, can and will protect me.

I ask for help to release all doubts and fears, for these vibrations make me vulnerable to dark force energies. I release all the old guilt, shame and feelings of unworthiness that I carry because of my past mistakes and participation in creating distorted energies.

TWO

THE DARK FORCES

We will now speak to you about the dark forces. There is much confusion as to who these beings truly are. Do these beings really exist or are they only archetypes? Do they just represent a state of mind consciousness on the Earth plane at this time?

We are here to continue the story to allow you to see how, when the energy, the God-given energy, the manifesting energy, was placed into the reflections, it took form and these forms became living entities. The dark forces are living entities that to this day still roam the Earth, as well as other planets and other planes of existence. These entities are not bound by time and space. They are free to roam.

Most of you have given power to these entities. They have incredible power, only because power was given to them. These entities became very cunning -- very cunning. They found many ways to get power from you, the Light-essence Beings. They found ways to play upon your vulnerabilities of guilt and shame, of fear and doubt and confusion. They found it so easy to enslave you. You were so loving, so trusting, so naive in nature.

We can still read the impressions of the memories of your thoughts. This is what you were thinking, "How could our loving God permit anything evil to be created? How could He? How could She? How could our God of Goodness and Love allow evil to roam the Earth plane, to roam the universes, to roam the different planes of existence, the different dimensions? Obviously, if God allowed these reflections, He must be angry with us. He must want to punish us. That's it, He wants to see us punished. We were bad and now He's allowing us to be punished. He is not the God we thought He was. He is not. He rules us with a strong arm. He is a dictator. We are not allowed to make any mistakes. We make one mistake and look what happens. Evil happens. We are not powerful. We thought we were powerful, but we are not. We have no power. The God of All, the God of Light, the God of Love, has cut us off. He is angry and He has cut us off. He cares not for our fate. He has allowed this evil to take hold. He has allowed us to stay in this darkness, this evil darkness. We are suffocating. Our power is being sucked from our very cores. Our God does not love us, His love is so conditional. We do one thing wrong and He cuts us off. He punished us. We must look away now, we must look away. We are no longer worthy. We are scum. We are nothing."

This attitude, my darling children, was fed to you by these entities to whom you yourselves had given energy; these entities we now term the dark brotherhoods, the dark forces. Once they found a way into you, to your essence, to your being, they began to play on your fears. They would feed your fears and your other vulnerabilities to confuse you. They would speak to you, sometimes through cordings, sometimes through aspects of themselves that they had integrated within you.

The dark forces constantly bombarded you with these thought forms, "Your God does not love you. Your God has deserted you. Ha-ha! He doesn't even care about you. He has left you here to die. He doesn't care about you, oh, you poor foolish children. You are so foolish. Look what you've done now. You've gotten yourself trapped. Oh, you are despicable. You children are despicable. He will never allow you back into His graces. He will not allow it. You are powerless now. You have nothing. You can do nothing on your own. What will you do? You are trapped."

"We have a plan. We can help you. We have power. We have lots of power and we can help you get your power back, but you will have to cooperate with us now. We have ways of helping you. What do you desire? Let us show you what is possible with our power. Let us show you what can be done with our power. Come along now. Your God has already left you. That God that you followed so blindly, that you had such faith in, He's already left you. So come along now. What are you going to do? You have no choice now. Come with us, we will help you out. We will clean you up and get you going again. We will help you manifest things that you have never manifested before. We will show you how to get power. We can show you."

THE CREATION OF LUCIFER

The first being created out of the reflection was the entity known as Lucifer. Many of you believe that Lucifer was an angel because he looked like Light. He looked like Light and yet he was not. He was merely a reflection of God's Light, to be looked at and learned from. He truly had no power in the beginning. You fed him power. You played with the reflection. He was created from your energy.

Again, you are not being judged. This is just a story to relay to you how dark beings came to be. It is to help you understand why they are still with you now. You, my children, created them. You gave life to the images you put into your reflections. These images had no life-force until you added energy to them. With your minds, your very powerful minds, you created this being known as Lucifer, who now, my children, has control over many beings on Earth. He has control over many powerful beings on Earth. The beings Lucifer controls are not just those who commit heinous crimes like raping and killing. Those beings are definitely being influenced, but Lucifer preys more on powerful beings, those who have power, those who have something to feed him, something to add to his repertoire, something he can play with and control, beings he can place on his game board and move around like pawns. So many of you have succumbed to Lucifer's game. You have made many contracts with him in times of need. Over time you have forgotten about these contracts, these agreements.

We are not saying this is hopeless. This is not hopeless. There is hope! For we see that many of you are attempting to wake up now. Many of you are trying to remember. God Himself has said, "Enough of your slumber, children. Enough. I miss you. I miss the joy when we created together. I miss your brilliance. I am a lonely God. So few seek Me. Most of you seek power and experiences, but few truly seek Me."

We see that there are beings on the Earth plane who are sincerely calling out and working towards reconnecting their Lights, but most get lost along the way, sidetracked along the way, because of old power lines and hook-ins with Lucifer. These power lines dissipate your power when you get to a point of waking up and truly seeing clearly. Your power gets pulled from you and you become sidetracked. You become fearful again.

Lucifer and his forces feed you the same subtle lies through old cordings, "This God is not attainable to you anymore. You can try all you want, but He will never allow you back. You are not worthy. You can try for twenty thousand more incarnations and you will still not be worthy enough for Him. So just forget about it, come on, forget about it. Remember, we have other things to do. Remember, we can control others. We know how to control others. You don't need to get the power you are seeking from God. You can do it by hooking into others and feeding off their Light. You know how easy it is to do that. We've done it in the past. We can do it again. We'll show you again. We'll do it again, then you will feel better. Just forget these ideas. Your God is not attainable."

Lucifer was protecting, and is still protecting, his own existence. For you see my darling children, without you Lucifer cannot exist. He owns no personal power. He has none of his own. He has taken and taken from all of those he has trapped and confused. All of you, at some time, have given up power to Lucifer.

AFFIRMATIONS

God's love for me is unconditional.

I no longer cooperate with the dark forces. I will not allow them to control me and feed off my energy and essence.

I break all past contracts and agreements with Lucifer and his cohorts. I release the old power lines and hook-ins I have with Lucifer.

God is attainable to me. He is waiting with open arms for my return. I am worthy of God's love and protection.

THREE

THE LAND OF PAN

Long ago, in the Land of Pan, there lived a young girl named Shameta. Shameta was a very great soul, confident and sure of her abilities and skills. She created whatever she desired just by using her mind. She knew how to draw to her all the people and situations she desired in her life. She was very happy creating each day, enjoying her creations and thanking God for the wonderful opportunity to enjoy such Earthly pleasure.

One day a handsome man came along and swept Shameta right off her feet. He seemed also a great soul and demonstrated spiritual prowess in the art of manifesting. "Shameta," he said one day, "Why don't we merge our energies together and become one great energy field? Think of what we could create. We might create a new universe. Come on, what do you say? We could be greater than God. We might even take over the Godhead and rule all of His creations. What do you say, do you love me enough to sacrifice yourself for my desire?"

Shameta was scared. She had never seen this side of her beloved before. She loved him with all her heart, but to do what he asked seemed to go against what she felt inside. She never before had to discern between right and wrong. She only knew happiness and joy. These new feelings that were created by her lover's request confused her and frightened her. She ran away but her lover ran after her. Since he was the stronger of the two he soon overcame her and forced himself on her. "If you won't merge with me in the way I want, I will just have to take your energy from you."

Shameta's eyes grew wide with terror. She had never before felt physical pain or known such violence. This man whom she had accepted as her spiritual counterpart was now heaving on her, wildly pumping his penis in and out, sucking the energy right out of her. She begged him to stop, but her cries just angered him more and he began hitting her with his fists until her face was bloody. Shameta surrendered and let go of her energy. He took what he wanted and left. "Now I will be the most powerful being in the universe. All others will have to obey my commands or I will destroy them with my power," he said as he strode off.

Shameta huddled in a ball whimpering. Her mind cried out, "My Father in Heaven, what happened? Why were You not watching over me? Why did You let this happen? What did I do to deserve this? Am I a bad person? Am I unworthy of Your love and protection?" So wounded was Shameta that she didn't wait to hear God's answer. She covered herself in mud and filth. She began to do and say things differently. Her trust in God was gone and so was her power to manifest. She began to steal food from others because she could no longer produce her own.

People began to hate her for her weakness. They spat on her and kicked her and each time they did this their power became a little less. No one was happy anymore. Everyone was worried and afraid, "If Shameta lost her power it could happen to us. She was so confident and sure of herself. Why don't we kill her, then we don't have to live with this constant fear."

A committee was formed and voted to stone Shameta to death on the grounds that she was now ugly and dirty and not worthy to live among them. An angry mob cornered Shameta and blow by blow took her life. Now the people could not look into each other's eyes anymore. They didn't like what they felt inside. They also became fearful that God would no longer listen to them and they stopped talking to Him. Their power had vanished, their hearts had hardened and there was no more joy in the Land of Pan. The beautiful trees began to shrivel and the sparkling lakes began to dry up. No food could be found anywhere and the people began to starve. They ate each other as a last resort until the great magical people of Pan no longer existed.

GOD speaks to the lost souls of Pan:

My dear beloved children, why have you closed your ears to Me? I have been calling you for so long. Your own fear and doubt prevented you from listening. The man disguised as Shameta's lover was none other than Lucifer. He has tricked you into feeling you are helpless against him. He has made you believe I am an uncaring God. This is not true. I do not punish you, you punish yourselves. Why do you not open your eyes and your ears and see Me and hear Me? I am always with you. I have always been available to you.

If Shameta would not have let her fear overcome her she could have called on Me immediately. I would have assisted her and saved her from falling under Lucifer's spell. Her fear stopped her from calling out to Me. I would have come. I always do and always will help those who call to Me. After Lucifer left, I could have still restored her power, but her anger and her guilt prevented her from seeing Me. I was standing right before her after she called, not to punish but to comfort, not to condemn but to heal. How many have turned away from My loving arms? How many still believe they are sinners and unworthy of My love? I tell you now that I love each one of you. I want to help you regain confidence in your abilities to create joy and peace and plentifulness.

Lucifer's spell has lasted too long. You have forgotten everything I taught you before you left My Presence seeking new experiences. I told you then and I tell you now, believe in Me. Restore your trust in My love. I will help you but you must ask with renewed faith, without doubt or fear, and believe with every part of your being that I can and will come through for you.

My dear children, peace will once again reign on your planet, but those who refuse My help now will not be able to stay. Those who refuse to wake up from Lucifer's spell will have to leave. I am taking over now. I have heard your Earth Mother's pleas for help and I now come to her and to those of you who are willing to receive Me.

AFFIRMATIONS

I know God is always with me and available to me. God always helps those who call to Him. He does not punish, He comforts. He does not condemn, He heals.

I no longer turn away from God's loving arms. I release the belief that I am a sinner and unworthy of God's love.

I believe in God. I restore my trust in God's love for me. I call upon You God with renewed faith, with no doubt or fear, and I believe with every part of my being that You can and will help me.

FOUR

THE LIGHT BEARERS' CALL TO ACTION

Some of you have worked very hard on your awareness and are no longer participating with Lucifer and his forces in the same way as the majority of the masses. And yet, even you aware ones are still under the illusionary belief that God is unattainable without much sacrifice, much pain and giving up. You believe it takes much austerity to even get a glance of His Goodness.

We read these impressions in your minds, "Oh, to even get a glance of God one must starve one's self of love. One must not be greedy and take anything for one's self. No, no. One must not do that. One must stay pure. One must stay separate and inside one's self. We know that there are energy seekers all around us. We know that energy vampires are waiting to suck our essence right out of us. So we will hide. We will hide away so they cannot touch us. We will not show them that we have power. We don't care about them. We only care about a chance, in some incarnation, some lifetime, to attain a glance of God. We cannot take the risk of dirtying ourselves. We will not take the chance of coming too close to any of these angry, consumed beings who claim they are Light. We know they are asleep. They are sound asleep. Why should we help them? Why should we? Look how they behave.

They behave so atrociously. They annoy us. Their energies annoy us. They do annoying things. Why would we want to associate with these beings? We don't want to. We want to stay to ourselves. We are special. We are not the same as them. We are special."

You, my children, have forgotten why you have come. You have forgotten that you were once as lost as these beings whom you claim are not the same. You claim these people, these beings, are not the same as you, that they are hopeless. You see them as only wicked, evil, cruel and gross. You only see the awful things they do and how you feel when you are around them. You have forgotten why you have come.

You have come to serve, to serve this beautiful God whom you remember so well in your hearts. You have forgotten that you have already attained God's glance, God's Eye. He is watching you, guiding you, protecting you. He is trying to help you complete this lifetime. He wants you to understand that you came here to complete this lifetime. You came here to finish up with this nonsense of coming and going and coming and going, from this realm of existence to that realm of existence, back and forth, here and there, but never coming Home. Your Father and your Mother are waiting with open arms, waiting for you to come and you never come. You still don't feel worthy. You don't feel ready, and yet you have already attained the Eye of God. It is burning within you, brightly burning, this eye of wisdom.

You have been asked to share your wisdom and to share your knowledge with those among you who are searching and seeking. They are searching and seeking and begging to be released from their bondage. They are asking over and over, "God, help us. We are so miserable. We don't know what to do. We don't know how to free ourselves from this Earth-bound existence. We don't even know why we want to, we only know we are not satisfied. We are not satisfied with the world we have created. We don't feel fulfilled."

"We have children. They are beautiful, God. We see glimpses of You in their eyes. We see sparks of wisdom in them, but we cannot remember this wisdom ourselves and then we confuse our children. We don't know how to teach them correctly and they become like us. That beautiful knowledge, that innocence we see in them dies when we show them our truth, or what we know as truth at our level of existence. Their eyes become dull and then we can't see You anymore, even in our children. We can't see You in our temples and in our churches. We can't see You in our pilgrimages. We can't find You anywhere. You must not exist. You must not even exist anymore."

"We look around and we see evil everywhere. It is in our government, it is in our churches. It's in ourselves. We are so confused. Oh, it is hopeless. Will someone give us some hope? Will someone share with us how to find Truth, the real Truth? We are so frightened that You don't exist anymore, God. Do You exist God? Could You show us a sign? Could you show us one small miracle to help us believe? We want to have faith, but we don't see anything happening that is good. We are so afraid."

You, my children, who know, who have the wisdom of God within you and the ability to see more clearly, have a responsibility to help those who are seeking to find Truth again. You must help them find the knowledge, the wisdom, the peace, the joy, the love and the fulfillment that they are lacking in their lives. Their lives are so meaningless.

You are being asked to step forward now and show yourselves. Show yourselves as the Beings of Light that you are. You were created in the same way as these beings. You are not special. You are not elite. You are hoarding beautiful essence, beautiful knowledge, that should be flowing freely from you to those who are calling out.

You are not being asked to push your ideas or your knowledge on others. This is not what we are saying. You are being asked to assist and share what you know with those who are seeking and coming forward now. This is a grave responsibility, for you know how easily people are swayed. You understand how easily their minds can be influenced. When they feel your power, they are very susceptible to whatever you are saying to them. They feel your essence and they think, "Oh, this person has something. There is something here. I will listen to this person. This person makes me feel secure. I will believe what this person tells me."

We are asking you to help these beings find their own power, to get back their own essence and reconnect to the Source of universal energy, the God Source. Show them the way! Show them the way back and then allow them their truth. Allow them to have their own truth. For you see, many of you have lost the ability to discern between what is real and what is not. You are so afraid that what you say may not be correct. You are so afraid that others may judge and condemn you, that others may say vicious, ugly things about you. And what if they are correct? What if you really don't know what you are talking about? What if all of your knowledge is not Truth? What will happen then?

We read your worried, confused minds, "I know I'll get lost again. I'll lose my chance to be with God. If I do it wrong I'll lose my chance to be with God. I'm going to keep to myself. That's it, I'll just work on me. That's it. I'll work on me. Me, me, me, me, me, me. That's it, me. I'll forget about everyone else. I don't need them. They are just going to get in the way and I'm going to get screwed up again. I'll just stay focused on me. I may speak to a few people if I know they are safe and accepting of me. But I'm not going to speak to anyone who is confused, anyone with doubt or fear, because I know they'll trip me up. I know that. They will trip me up, they've done it before. Every time I've tried to help in the past I've gotten tripped up. No, I'm going to stay to myself this time, myself and a few close friends that I know accept me. That's good enough, isn't it God? You certainly don't want me to do more than that. It's for me to work on me, right? I know that one. It's for me to work on me."

GOD speaks:

I weep. I feel sadness. I feel remorse. I feel lost sometimes Myself, lost and bewildered. What more can I do? What more can I do to show you that I am accepting, that I am understanding, that I am not judging your every word, your every movement, your every action, your every interaction? I am not judging you. I am waiting for you to give up these old fears. I am asking you to give them up now. I am asking you to give them up and help Me assist those who are calling. Help Me. Help Me assist those who want to be saved.

For you see, My children, the time is short. Soon your Earth Mother is going to expel all beings who do not have the knowledge, the intuition, the freedom, to know how to create safety. She is not going to be selective. She is not choosing who can stay and who must go. You are choosing this fate yourselves.

This is the time to help those who truly desire to be helped. They are calling out, they are asking. You must hear them. You must come out of your own limited existence, your own self-centeredness and understand that you are all of the same essence. You are all of the same essence. You are not different, you are just more awake. It is your responsibility to help these beings. It is the way to further your own spiritual growth. You have agreed to do this. Why are you so afraid to keep your agreement? Why? It is because these dark forces tell you that you will not succeed. These forces add energy and intensify your every doubt, your every fear. They attack you and scare you. They cling to you, and yet My children, if you were clear, if you were crystal clear within yourselves, there would be nothing for these beings to hold onto. They cannot attach to Truth, to love, but they can attach to anger, guilt, fear, shame, lust -- here's a huge one My children, lust. Lust after essence. Lust after essence that does not belong to you. Many are lusting after another's essence. This is the reason behind the contracts that contribute to the cordings you have with each other. Contracts, contracts. "You are mine. I own you. You are mine and these children are mine. You are mine and you must not look at another."

Where did this come from? You are not owned. You are not owned by anyone. You are free Beings of Light. You are allowed to flow and shift and change. Do you not remember how with just a thought you would change into whatever you desired? There was no desire to hold on to any particular form. No, when you were done you let it go, you just let it go. It was fun. You enjoyed it. You learned from it. You experienced and explored with a form and then you let it go and became free again. You did not stay in any form longer than the enjoyment lasted. When the enjoyment was over you returned back to your natural state, your natural state of Lightness. But now you have locked up so much of your essence. You are trapped in your bodies. You feel so insecure being trapped in your bodies that you need others to promise to stay with you, to never leave you. "Stay with me. You can never leave me, never ever. You cannot leave me, you are mine now."

This comes because, My children, you are so insecure. You are holding on to others, many others. "You are my friend, you are my husband, you are my teacher." You are holding on and each time you do this you bind that person with what has been identified as a cording. You bind that person with that intense desire to hold them, to possess them, to keep them for yourself. You do it with your children, "You are mine." You immediately cord with your children. You bind them and then through these cordings you convince them that they are not free.

Your children look in the sky and see the airplanes and the birds. They see that things can fly and they understand, "We can do that!" But you parents say, "No, you have bodies, you can't fly. It's not possible, don't think about that." You have trained your children to limit their thinking. You have encouraged them to shut down what they came in knowing as Truth, "We could fly like that airplane. We could fly like that bird. We could shrink ourselves small enough to fit into that play car and drive it around. We could do that, we know we could." And as soon as the child begins expressing his thoughts, the parent, the caregiver is so concerned, "Oh, don't have those wrong ideas. You can't do that."

You have shut down your beautiful children! You have shut them down and helped them stay stuck in this Earth-bound truth, this man-made truth. You do this every day. You do it with each other. One begins to come forward and starts to feel, "Wait, wait, I feel something alive and flowing within me. I feel that perhaps there is a possibility I may have been wrong." And right away everyone who is corded to this awakening person starts to bombard him with negative thoughts, "No, no, you know that's not possible. It's not possible. You can't do that. Don't even think about it. You can't do that." Soon after these thoughts are sent, the newly awakened person begins to mistrust his feelings. "Oh, I don't know what I was thinking about, but I sure feel miserable now. When that energy was flowing I felt so good, I felt so alive, I felt so free. I felt so much hope. Now I feel tired and angry. I feel despondent. I'm depressed. I'm so depressed. Only a moment ago I felt good. That was wrong, that was wrong. What I was thinking isn't possible. It can't be possible."

The ANCIENT HIERARCHY speaks:

We are here this day to continue the inspiration, the inspiration that will lead to many souls awakening and many beings who are already awake to come to action. You are being called to action and fast movement is needed. Fast movement is needed to save souls. We are not trying to frighten you or give you the impression that if you do not heed our messages you will be punished, for that is not the case.

We are calling you to remember the agreements you made before taking this lifetime. Before taking this lifetime you committed to come to Earth, to serve, to help, to remember who you are and how to assist others in finding their truth. If you do not cooperate you will also leave the planet, for there will be no reason for you to stay. Those who hoard anything will have to leave. All of those who hoard energy will have to leave. Even material things are but made of energy forms, energy thought forms. Those who hoard will be taken off, for the Earth Mother has now declared that she will only support those who are willing to share and flow together and work together as one unit, one life force.

Do not fear, it is not your destiny to be lost. It is your destiny to return to the Godhead from whence you came, from where you originated. This is the fate of every man on Earth; to return to the Godhead, to return to the origin, going back, back, all the way back to the very beginning, the Source of Creation.

So many are frightened by this idea, "No, we don't want to hear that. We don't want to go back, we want to go on, we want to experience more. We want to experience greater pleasures. We don't want to go back. That sounds frightening. We are afraid to go back. We know we are supposed to want to be with God, but it sounds boring. It sounds very boring. Going back into what? Merging into what? Becoming a non-person, becoming a pool of what? Liquid Light? We don't understand, we truly don't understand. We are afraid to go back to Spirit because we are afraid it's not going to be what we had hoped for. We have expectations of glory, of tables filled with sumptuous foods, and men and women to be sexual with, and no AIDS and no disease and no lack of anything. We want to be able to feed our appetites. We have strong appetites here. We are afraid our appetites will not be fed. We need to be fed. It is probably best that we just keep coming back here, because at least we know that we can feed our appetites here. We can be sexual here, we can eat food here, we can create and if we are lucky we can create beautiful things and we can own them and use them."

"Oh, it's a lot of work though. It's a lot of work to keep all of our appetites fed here, but we really can't trust going back into nothing, because if we go back into nothing we might not exist, right? And we want to exist, we truly want to exist. We are afraid of dying. My gosh, we are afraid of dying because we won't exist and then what fun will we have? At least now we exist and when we die we will go to a place that exists also. It has form, there are people there, we do things and then we come back here again and then we can start working on our appetites. Maybe we will start to control them more. 'Next time I won't eat so much and I won't be so fat. I won't be so lusty next time, I won't. Maybe I'll be born into a monastery or something, that's it and that will help me get those appetites under control. Hmmm, but then what?'"

"All of the spiritual teachings talk about going back into the One. No, we better just keep trying it our way. We know that our way at least has form, something to hold on to, something we can taste, something we can smell, something we can touch, yeah, that's better. I guess I'm not ready to go back into the One. I am afraid I won't exist anymore. I'm sorry God, if what You want is to pull me back so I don't exist, I guess I really don't want to come. I guess I don't. I will just keep taking my chances with these incarnations on Earth and other places where I can at least know I will exist. I am, I am, I am, at least I am something, but I don't know what You are God, and I am afraid to find out, for I'm afraid I won't exist."

AFFIRMATIONS

My Father and Mother are waiting with open arms to welcome me Home.

I am ready and worthy to return to God.

I am willing to step forward now, as a Being of Light, and share my knowledge and wisdom.

God loves, accepts and understands me. I release the fear that He judges my every word, movement and action.

I am not owned by anyone. I am a free Being of Light who is allowed to flow and shift and change.

I stop holding onto others out of insecurity and binding them to me with cordings. I allow us all to be free.

I share my knowledge, energy and material possessions with those in need. I am willing to share and flow together with the Earth and her inhabitants. We all work together as one unit, one life force.

It is my destiny to return to the Godhead from where I originated. Going back into the One does not mean losing my identity. It means reconnecting to the Source of Goodness and Love.

FIVE

LUCIFER'S ENTRAPMENTS

Oh, the fears you hold, my children, because of the lies that have been told to you by Lucifer and his forces. Lucifer, the master persuader, the master illusion-builder has told you so many lies. He has told you that there is nothing for you with God.

Lucifer tells you, "If you return to God, you will not exist, so go ahead, reconnect. Just reconnect and beat it on back to Him, but then what will you have? God tells you, 'Come merge back into Me.' God just wants your power. He wants to control and consume you. He wants to take you back within Himself and then have more for Himself. He wants to control you. Don't let Him do that."

"Now, if you stay with me I will show you how to be independent and in control of your life. You can create whatever you want. I'll show you how to do it. You are greedy. I know you're greedy. You want more, more, more. You're never satisfied. That is your nature. You're never satisfied. You need me. You need me because you cannot be satisfied. You are hungry over and over again. You want sex over and over again. You want pleasure over and over again. You are just plain old greedy. You are insatiable, your appetites are out of control. Oh, you need me, you certainly need me. Now, that God of Light and Goodness, as you call Him, is only going to consume you and then you won't exist anymore. So if I were you I wouldn't go back to Him. If you go there, it's all over."

"If you stay with me I can guarantee you another birth when your physical body dies. I can guarantee it. If you make a contract with me I can guarantee you another place, another body, and you can continue right where you left off. Doesn't that sound good? You will exist. Doesn't that sound like what you want? At least you exist. At least you know there is something you can hold onto, there is a form you can hold onto. You're secure then, right? You're secure. You'll have a body and I am telling you right now that when you lose that one I can get you another one. We can keep creating bodies for you."

"I know it's getting a little crowded here, I know that, but that's okay because there are other places that we can go. There are other planets that we can go to. I have other planets just waiting for you. I have ships. I have spaceships that can pick you up. I am in charge of many fleets of spaceships. We can pick you up and take you to another location. You can continue on."

"Ummm, there's one thing you are going to have to do though. You are going to have to promise to let me work through you whenever I need to. I won't do it all the time, but there definitely will be times when I need to use your vehicle to get my way, to continue my ploys, to greater my own existence. I need to have you agree that I can work through you whenever I want to. Is that okay? I think it sounds like a pretty good deal. I think it sounds like a great deal. Think about what you get, eternal existence, because I am going to guarantee you a body as many times as you want one. Um, there is a little clause to this contract -- it may not always be the body you want."

"I cannot guarantee you great beauty and perfect health. I can't do that one, I'm sorry. But at least you will have a body and you know if you don't like something we have ways of changing it. I can show you how to change it. I can show you how to surgically remove parts you don't want, diseased parts. We can fix that body up. And if you don't like the way it looks, we can change that too. We've got some great methods down here on Earth that we have developed. We can make your nose bigger or smaller. We can take fat off your stomach and suck it out of your hips. We can get rid of those wrinkles around your eyes. In case you don't get the perfect form that you wanted, we can pretty much do anything that you need. Don't worry about it. Just put your faith in me, Lucifer, because I have a lot of control over the medical society. Most of the doctors know what I want from them and they cooperate. Don't worry if your body is diseased or ugly or deformed. We can take care of it for you. We have great methods of surgery and drug treatment."

"Don't forget your end of our agreement though. You have to allow me into your body whenever I want it. It's an automatic, I don't warn you. I don't say, 'Excuse me, I need to come into your body and use you so I can get what I want from the people you're dealing with.' No, that's not how it is done. Be very clear with this clause of the contract. It says, 'I can come into your body whenever I want to, without warning, without asking again. I can just do it.' Do you understand that? Just so we're clear on that one. Don't get any ideas about changing your mind because once you agree to this it's permanent, written in cement. I can come and go as often as I choose, whenever I feel like it and you must allow it -- okay? You can have a body again and I can come and go. Just so we're clear."

Lucifer is very cunning and wise, for he has much wisdom. He attained this wisdom by studying the energy patterns within each one of you. Lucifer attained his cunningness by deciphering minute particles of energy within your brains. He is so clever because he has been able to tap into the genetic coding of the human entity. He knows how it works and also how to distort it for his advantage. When you are being filled with spiritual inspiration, Lucifer knows how to trigger from within tiny minute portions of your brain that will then misfire the signals that are being sent to you, making it then difficult to process new information. Your old habit patterns of thinking will be sustained.

Lucifer receives this knowledge by merging himself with you. He has acquired the knowledge of all of your experiences without having to live them himself by merging his energy with you, and you have allowed this, my children. Because you have allowed it, he is free to come and go as often as he chooses. He has created bodies within you that are conducive to his energy forms so he can easily fit right inside you. We say forms because he has more than one form.

Lucifer has been able to decipher the DNA within you. He knows how to manipulate it to get control over your vehicles. He is a very clever entity and this cleverness has cost each one of you dearly, for you have surrendered much of your essence to him. You have surrendered your bodies to be biologically deformed at times to suit his needs, to be disease-ridden at times to suit his needs, for he is into pain and suffering as a way of control.

He controls you through this pain and suffering and when you are down and out Lucifer comes around and says, "Hey, I can fix this for you. What is it you need? I have power. If you align with me I can help you. I can help you get out of this mess that you're in. Are you in a financial mess? I can help you with that. I know how to create money. All you have to do is say yes to me and I will turn you on to the right people, who I am controlling of course, who will give you the job or the opportunity or just give you the money if that's what you want. I can arrange that, but then I own you, understand that. I own you and your vehicle. You must allow me to come and go as I please, and understand that I will not be satisfied with just one visit. I will come and go whenever I want to."

We can see you struggling with this information. We can hear you thinking, "How can we believe that we have allowed ourselves to be overtaken by Lucifer? How do we know that this is not Lucifer now speaking through this channel?" Children, feel the purity of the energy that flows into you as you read this material. Feel the Light permeating through every cell.

Feel the transformation happening within you as you open to this energy, the changes which feel confusing, yet freeing. Continue to notice all of these feelings as you read on, and know this transformational energy is coming from God.

God will help you if you but believe in Him again, but you must let go of these dark energies that have penetrated you and built within you their own vehicles. You must discard them at this time for God to be able to effectively work with you. You must be freed up to return to your original essence. You have much essence that needs to be retrieved so you can once again be whole and complete and at One with the God Energy. Then all is possible; all can be achieved.

Lucifer has deceived you over and over, and each time he does so, you struggle with your own fears, your own doubts and vulnerabilities. When these vulnerabilities surface, instead of giving up, you must move forward knowing, "This is not Truth. Truth feels wonderful. Truth feels alive, life-giving. This feels like death. What feels like death is not God, for God is life. God is energy flowing. This is stuckness, this is Lucifer's doing. This is my fear feeding these forces to hold me back. I will not allow it. I will not. I will call out strongly to the Beings of Light to assist me. I will call on God Himself to come to my rescue. Save me now, I believe in You. I will do my part. I will claim back my essence, my power. These dark beings will no longer control my vehicle. I will not allow it. I am aligned with You, God. I am One with You. I am One with You and I exist. I will exist for others to see and know it is possible to be aligned with You, it is possible to be joyful and to give and receive love. For God, You are love and I am love along with You. I am love. The power within me receives You now. The power within me releases all darkness now. The power within me will accept only Truth, only Truth."

GOD speaks:

I have imparted to you sacred sounds (mantras) that have been delivered throughout the ages by my messengers. These sacred sounds bring Light to those who have lost hope, to those who have lost essence. These sacred sounds trigger the ancient memories of when we roamed the Earth plane together, as One, connected as one unit, energy flowing from Me, the Source, coming into you, the Ray of Light, and manifesting through your earth body. I urge you to seek out my sacred sounds and use them to activate these ancient memories, my dear children, and to remember what is possible and how to achieve beauty, joy, fulfillment, balance and harmony between all beings and forces of Nature.

Your Earth Mother has been so abused. She is so tired and worn out. She has been stripped of her valuable assets. She has been looted, raped and beaten over and over again. And even though her pain is great, she is not willing to give up and surrender her spiritual essence to the dark forces who play in the hearts of men and trigger them to greed, to hoarding and to continually abuse her. She is strong in her spirituality and is trying to align and merge now with Me, to help her achieve balance and bring her into the high vibrational frequency needed to assist her healing and transformational process. After her transformation, no beings will be allowed on her surface that hold any negative energy. Only those who are pure in thought and deed will be received by her. Those who are aligned with my God-Force Energy will be welcomed and supported by her.

Your Earth Mother has secrets hidden away where many have not been able to penetrate. She has secret holdings that she will release to those of God-Mind, and they will have abundance on Earth. She is willing to share with those of you who are able to align with us, and even in this time of confusion and chaos, you will have prosperity and abundance in all forms. But my children, she will not release these secrets to anyone who harbors dark energies.

She has made a firm commitment to do whatever it takes to release every dark energy within herself, and she will cry for those who needlessly give up their essence to the dark forces. She will mourn their loss, for she loves all. But yet, she is the Mother, and the Mother must survive for those children who want to change, who want to learn, who want to thrive in balance and alignment with Me and creation. Her vision and intention is clear. She is letting go of all the feelings of unworthiness that arise within her again and again. She clears out these doubts and releases them by whatever means possible, for she knows that these doubts are entrapments of Lucifer's. She is working on releasing all of her fears so she can accept the Energy I am willing to shower on her, to spark her to new life and renewed strength. In order for

Me to assist her in changing her energy form, she is relinquishing the whirling vortexes of dark energies that hold her from within. You, my children, must follow your Earth Mother's example and work as diligently as she is to free yourselves from everything that is holding you back from receiving my Light.

The ANCIENT HIERARCHY speaks:

Lucifer's ploy is to create as many powerlines as possible between himself and vehicles of power in order to achieve great feats and have leverage in the game he has master-minded, for he has turned Mother Earth into an intricate game board. The way the game is structured, the only players who can win are players who have succumbed to Lucifer. There are no openings for Truth. There are no openings for God. However, this game is only on your Mother's surface and this is not the core of who she is. She has allowed you to play this game with Lucifer, but now her own core essence is being threatened and she can no longer allow it. She is going to erupt and break up the pieces of this game board. With the help of the Almighty God-Force, she will break up these pieces and Lucifer's game will be destroyed. His game will be destroyed and in its place, my dear children, will come the Universal Plan for peace and fulfillment for all beings and creations of God, from the mineral kingdom, to the vegetable kingdom, to the animal kingdom, to the highest kingdom on Earth, humankind. Balance and love and alignment with the Almighty Father and Mother will once again be restored. This, my children, will be so awesome, so magical. Once again we will flow together in perfect harmony,

Spirit and Nature dancing together.

Lucifer has a strong hold on the Earth and has banded together many beings from many places to assist him. He has spacial invasions going on continuously throughout the Earth plane and other planets he is trying to gain control over. These spacial beings are non-loving in essence. Their essence is not the same as those created from the Source. You humans who have true soul essence were created from the Source of God, the Source of Goodness. You are One with this Source. These spacial entities who invade your planet and invade your bodies are not made of God Essence. They are manipulated essences, created by Lucifer. Lucifer has taken much of your essence, learned the intricacies of the DNA and from this has created many different species of beings whom he totally controls.

Now children, understand that there are also extraterrestrials of Light and love that have been created by the God of Goodness. These Beings dwell in other dimensions and are One with God and serve Him.

God Himself has created many beautiful spaceships to carry His own loving essence in formed Beings of Light to patrol the universes and tune-in to frequencies of crisis. Their missions are to serve you, to support you, to free you and help you return Home again. These beings perform these duties willingly because they know no greater joy than seeing more beings of God Essence come Home again. When we speak of you coming Home, we do not mean we will physically transport you to another place in another dimension. No. This coming Home means going inward until you reach the very core of your existence and find the thread that holds you connected at all times to the life-giving Energy, and then reconnecting your minds to this thread of Light, that will lead you into the greater part of yourself. There is so much of you that you do not know. So much is lying dormant. You must connect with this thread, this thread of God-giving Energy within you, and travel this thread back to your High Self, the High Self which knows Truth. You must reconnect your mind to this High Self and know Truth again.

The dark forces would like you to stay separate from your High Self. They would like to see your energy flow into the circuits that they have created within you, for once your energy is flowing through these circuits you have little control over your thinking. You will think the thoughts that are sent to you. Also, your own negative thoughts that you work so hard to shift and dissipate are reinforced by these forces and you will rethink them and rethink them and you will stay stuck. You will stay stuck because you will not get past these thought forms.

The energy bodies that Lucifer has so cunningly built within you to receive him are energy bodies that feel like light. They feel so comfortable and familiar to you. These energy bodies activate when your doubts and fears surface. As soon as you begin to release your doubts and fears these energy bodies come forward and begin to vibrate your thought forms into vortexes. The vortexes circulate your thought forms and hold them in place within the chakras. These vortexes become very strong magnetic fields that hold your thoughts, your doubts and fears in place so they cannot be released, and you remain stuck.

Lucifer created these vortexes by studying essence he collected from many of you over time. He has created circuitry in your energy bodies that misfire when you are ready to claim your power.

What an intricate operation this is. We marvel at the ingenuity of this being Lucifer, who keeps you stuck when you are ready to release what is holding you back! Think of it, when you are ready to release what is holding you back, this force gets activated. What a cunning, cunning plan.

We are not revealing these Truths to frighten you or to make you feel hopeless. We are here to assist you and show you how to release these energy bodies that fit inside you so well that it feels like one is dying to give them up. Children, unless these old forms die, you will not be able to experience the beautiful spiritual rebirth of who you truly are, of who you always have been, you will not be able to reconnect to the God Source and manifest all you deserve and need.

Those who are manifesting without doing this work are pawns of Lucifer. Some have awareness of these energy bodies within them but they are not willing to relinquish the material gain they have been able to acquire by aligning with the dark forces. They are not willing to give it up because they do not want to go through the learning lessons, the remembrances and the surrendering that must be done. Total surrendering must be done to truly align and again become One with God. You must surrender, my children. You must surrender everything within you that is not of original God Essence.

Most of you will feel as though you are dying. You will feel as though there is nothing left.

Again we say to you, unless these dark force interferences go, you will never reunite with the Godhead. Only a few have merged back into the One. There are many places to go and many illusions to be shattered as to what is Light and what is God. It is not as difficult as it seems.

What makes it seem difficult is that the dark forces are playing on you and telling you, "This is not attainable. You cannot do this. Remember what happened when you tried it before? You got all confused. You abused your power. You hurt others. You lied. You cheated. You raped. You will get out of control again. At least when you are aligned with us you are controllable. Of course, we control you, but you are controllable. Alone you will get into the worst mischief and terrible messes, just as you did way back when you were first given your Free Will. What did you do? You messed up. And now you want to try it again? I don't think you're ready, do you? I think it's safer for you to stay with us. We can at least assure you existence and that's what you really want. You want to exist."

BEINGS CREATED BY LUCIFER

Many of you are in doubt that anyone besides God can create. It is time for you to understand that there are ways of taking your essence and creating new life forms from it. Look at what is being done in laboratories today. The sperm of one and the egg of another are brought together in test tubes and life is created. This has been happening for eons on the dark spaceship we call the "Clinic." We call the Clinic a dark spaceship not because it is black in color, but because it has no alignment with the God Energy.

The Clinic is run by a group of beings who have been followers of Lucifer for many lifetimes, many spans of existence. These followers of Lucifer dwell on this ship and create life forms that have no original God Essence in them. These created life forms are puppets of Lucifer. He uses them to manipulate, to seduce and to conquer others to give up their God Essence to him. His army, as we call it, is very vast. He has also created beings that dwell on different planes of existence. Lucifer and his forces have cloned many beings from Earth beings, human forms, and has ordered these clones to travel to Earth and be placed in positions that will benefit him.

Lucifer now has footholds in all major religions, in the medical society and in the governments of many countries because of these implanted beings. These implanted beings do not carry God's vibration. They speak well, look good, bleed if cut and cry if hurt because they have programmed emotional responses. Lucifer and his cohorts have studied the emotional body carefully and have duplicated its normal functioning and programmed this function into the implanted beings.

Lucifer and his cohorts have developed very sophisticated technologies that can change the form of essence. On the Clinic they can take the essence of a cow and change it into the essence of a human. This changeover of essence has been going on for some time. Animals have been taken and converted into forms that are human-like and placed in positions where they will radiate energy that attracts to them more of the same.

These created beings of Lucifer are grouping up. Some have formed secret organizations and their group vibration is causing havoc and disturbance among those who are trying to harmonize and align with God's Energy. These secret organizations perform rituals that create strong negative fields of energy. These negative energy waves nauseate those who are sensitive. These cloned beings hold their meetings in hillsides and countrysides where they will not be visible. These places are familiar to them since they once roamed these areas as animals. Their natures are still instinctual and yet they follow the programming of their master, Lucifer. When they are called they come together in great orgies, performing rituals using sexual acts and mind-altering drugs which give them the false sense of being very powerful and important. Remember, these beings are not truly humans. They are cloned from other essence that originally belonged to animals or has been taken from others and is now changed to obey the vibrations sent to them by their masters on the Clinic. It is not only animal-like beings that band together in herds that have been cloned, but also distinguished individuals who have been stalked and manipulated and drawn to the Clinic.

Many doctors are cooperating with the dark forces by taking essence from people they operate on and then turning the stolen essence over to the beings on the Clinic. Most are not conscious of their participation or programming to follow the instructions given to them that they received during their own abductions. Many have exchanged energies and made contracts with Lucifer to be the ones to gather God-given Essence from those who are sick, from those who are dying, from those who come to them in need. The doctors who have made contracts with Lucifer have been given much power over others and are very dangerous. Since these beings have no compassion in their hearts, butchery is widespread. They truly do not care what happens to others, they are only concerned with themselves. They need to be separated out from those who truly are of the Light and are here to heal.

Many of you have made contracts with Lucifer and the beings he has created on some plane of existence. Many of these contracts were not made on Earth, but when you come into your Earth body these contracts are still potent and valid. The contracts you have made with these beings need to be broken, canceled and dissolved, and the energy of the beings and the contracts need to be released from your bodies. We know that many questions are forming in your minds. We will work patiently with you to help you understand these concepts, for the mind opens slowly to concepts that have been hidden for so long.

Most of the beings who allow dark energies into them are not aware that they are being influenced. When someone is overtaken with dark energies you will not see any God Energy flowing from their eyes or their hearts. Look to the eyes always. The eyes have been called the windows into the soul. Look to the eyes and see if it is God Essence shining through or the dark, cold harshness of Lucifer's energy. The dark forces work very hard to sway people to allow them in, and then they control their mind power.

We have known about the implants that have been placed in humans for some time now. We have also known about the starship called the Clinic. We have been calling forth the Lightworkers who are willing to speak out about the dark forces and the many ways they are interfering. We are asking them to wake up the public to the awareness of what is happening, allowing them the opportunity to decide if they want to cooperate with these dark forces or align with the God Essence and become whole again. It is still a choice. Free Will still prevails.

True Light Beings never interfere with your Free Will choices and do not manipulate in any way. You must be able to recognize those who carry dark force energy and understand how they work so that you can once again have real choice as to how you live your life. Do you want to be manipulated and controlled or do you want to take back your power, be empowered and move forward in your spiritual evolution? With awareness there is always choice.

We hear many calling out now, asking desperately to be released from the bondage and the constant burden of fighting against the impulses being sent to follow the bidding of the dark forces. Many of you go into shear terror at the mere mention of dark forces. You defensively state, "You have created the existence of these dark forces with your minds and you are giving these thoughts power and energy. We do not do that. We are not controlled. We feel sorry for you because you are battling something that you need not battle. If you do not focus on the dark forces they will go away, they won't exist."

This attitude, my children, is caused by terror. Those of you who have this attitude know the terror of being alone, of being separate from God. You have allowed the dark forces to convince you that you are with God as long as you ignore the happenings around you. You are told that those who notice the dark energies are evil themselves. You are told this over and over by many of your spiritual leaders, "Those that notice the darkness are on the wrong path. They have fallen off the path, they have lost it. They are no longer going to receive God." My children, this is not true.

Most of you have given up hope of ever being reunited with the true Creator. Your concepts of God are confused. You mantra and pray and perform rituals which attune you to certain deities, aspects of God. You worship these deities and see them separate from yourself. You have forgotten that you are also a God-Being created from original God Essence. You are God, therefore, you are worthy to be reunited with more of Yourself.

You are not reuniting with your God Energy because you are being controlled and manipulated. This is so important to understand. One must see the darkness and the Light, one must see it all to be able to properly discern and choose where to focus energy. Ignoring a problem does not make it go away -- look at your world. My children, it is time to take off your rose-colored glasses, time to widen your range of vision and see what is really going on. Your world is like a movie set that you are mistaking to be real. You must look deeper now, to behind the set and see who is directing the movie. Take back your power and be brave enough to see.

There are many forms of evil on your plane of existence at this time. These forms now need to be identified and dealt with, for people are being used and abused at levels that are truly disgusting. As we have already stated, there are many beings now present on your Earth who are feeding on your energy and essence. We have also made you aware that these beings enter through your vulnerabilities. They enter through cordings that were created long ago when these forces tricked you into believing they were of the Light. These beings looked like Light. They emanated power that made you believe that by giving your energy to them you would again become powerful. We have already told you how the traps were laid. We now want to help you have clear understanding of how these forces became vital. For you see, dear ones, these forces intend to take over the soul essence of all of God's creations.

Lucifer's dark spacial beings are preying heavily on humans at this time. They have devised a way of entering through your genetic codes and have created many distortions in your DNA. These dark spacial entities are not working with agreements. They have found a way to enter human beings at birth. Many integrate and merge with the original soul essence during the birthing process. They enter children quite easily and stay with them for their entire life span.

EVASION, THE DARK ENERGY SOURCE

All formed dark energies come out of the same source, an energy force-field we call Evasion. Just as you have come out of the Source of Love and Light as Rays, all of the formed evil entities we are discussing have come out of this dark source of energy named Evasion. In certain ways this Evasion energy is very similar to the God Energy. It will create formed energies from the mental images that are placed within its power source.

But, because the Evasion energy has no power of its own, it is not like the God Energy. The Source of God is ever-evolving. It is like a generator that just keeps generating more and more and more. God does not need to be fueled by anything to keep creating. God never needs to be fed. The God Energy just keeps going and going and keeps creating and creating. As His creations go out to explore and experience, it is by choice that they flow in and out of the Godhead.

But this Evasion, this dark energy force-field, works exactly in the reverse. It has to draw. It needs to be fed or it will no longer exist. It started out as just a reflection of God's Light. Just as the sun casts a shadow, this was just a shadow of the Source. The Rays of Light went to explore the shadow, played in it, gave it energy and found creating with it interesting and different. Do you see the connection? The Light actually drew into the shadow. Since the Rays of Light are being fed by the God Source and they are now connected into the Evasion energy also, it is like God Himself is feeding this Evasion energy. Everything that is created by the Evasion energy is created from beautiful God Essence that has been manipulated and changed from its original intent. (See Diagram 1)

The God Source does not want to be used in this way. The abuse of energy has gotten completely out of control. The Evasion energy is always hungry and has to keep finding new ways to feed all of its creations, the dark entities that have come out of it. The larger it becomes, the more it needs. It is not just taking essence from the original beings who played in it, now it has found ways to take essence from newborn babies, from animals, from trees and plants. It is because of this abuse of Free Will that God has decided to intervene, but the needed actions must be carefully implemented. If God would just cut off all flow of His Energy to stop feeding the Evasion energy, all the beings who are hooked into it would perish. What He is trying to do is wake up the consciousness of those who are being controlled and used by the dark force energies and truly are not aware of their participation. One must have awareness to have choice.

Those who give up the darkness now will be saved. Those who continue to hold on to it will be destroyed along with it. It is because of God's great compassion and love for all of His creations that such tremendous effort is being made to give everyone an opportunity to align with Him again.

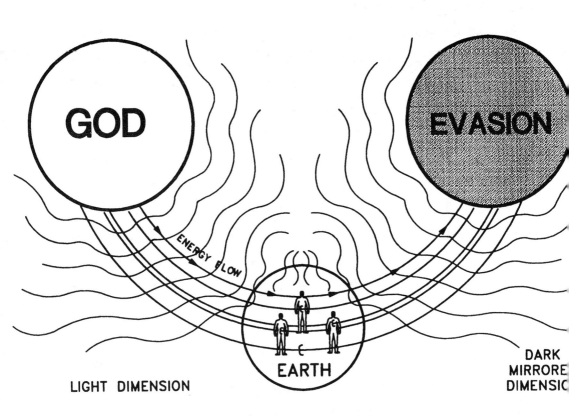

DIAGRAM 1

ASHTAR speaks:

We have already identified many beings who are connected to the Extraterrestrial Conspiracy that is going on. You need to understand that out of Evasion different energy forms are created in different dimensions.

There are many extraterrestrials that are visiting your planet mainly to explore and observe. These are not the higher dimensional beings that plan to overtake the Earth. It is this plan that we are determined to stop. They know of our existence and that we have plans to stop them. There is truly a 'star war' going on and the Earth is one of the planets being battled over at this time.

The game is played differently from what is depicted in your movies and in your stories. It is not with spaceships and missiles that the battling is being done, but rather through energy forces and energy fields that need to be blocked and stopped and destroyed. A mere missile will not do that. These stories are distortions and are coming from the minds of men and not from the true reality of the upper dimensions.

There is space travel through the dimensions and each shift brings about a new game, a new set of rules that need to be followed. We understand it is very difficult for you to comprehend how all of this can exist. That is why we have given the name "Evasion" to this massive energy force. It is evasive. It evades your minds and because of that it is the most dangerous force of all.

The Clinic, the dark spacial vehicle we have spoken about, can travel the different dimensions. The minds of men have helped create openings in the different dimensions. Some have cooperated out of curiosity for the spacial realms, feeling it is a great honor to bring such energies to the Earth. Some of you have made contracts with the dark forces.

This vast energy field, Evasion, has now broken through all the dimensions and there is no blocking or stopping it. It now has a tight hold on your Earth. Evasion is like a grim reaper who has gripped its fingers around your Earth and has claimed her for itself. It is ready to gobble up all of the available essence, not caring who is good and who is bad. It has no discernment or caring about its activities. You and the Earth are just viewed as essence to be consumed, and in such a vulnerable state you are easy pickings. Evasion is now coming down, going through all the dimensions, grasping everything and seeping in everywhere.

There are many extraterrestrials that act as mere drones for the dark hierarchy of beings on the Clinic. Many of these drone-like beings are on constant assignment to collect essence from different beings on different planets. It is not only planet Earth that is being preyed on, there are other beings inhabiting other planets who are also being preyed on in this same way. The Clinic has been collecting specimens, working with the genetic codes of many different beings and creating new beings from these original essences. They are also experimenting with the essences of the planets themselves in an effort to create environments that will suit their master plan.

Lucifer and his cohorts plan to create a universe that will consistently feed and sustain the needs of their energy forces. They are, in a sense, trying to recreate creation to fit their needs. This is a frightening plan to those of us who are watching. Understand we are watching, but we are watching from the dimensions of Light. We do not dwell in these dark reflections. We have sent volunteers to explore these dark realms and communicate information to us so we can figure out a way to stop them.

Evasion is like a huge machine that just keeps eating and eating and becomes larger and larger. Now the Godhead Itself is threatened. We must take action at this time. The only course of action is to draw back into the Godhead all of the Light Beings and planets for safety. We cannot allow creation to continue to be disturbed.

When God chooses to draw back all of His Light, a tremendous implosion of energy will be created. We realize that this is a hard concept for your minds, but try to understand that such an implosion of energy will push the Godhead back, creating a void between all of creation that is attached to the Godhead and moves with It, and all of creation that is not connected and is left behind. The void will be created by the sheer impact of so much energy being reversed in flow. God will pull with Him all of the beings and planets that have been freed from the Evasion energy and have aligned with His Energy. After the void is created, all of those left in the grip of Evasion will be left forever, because this void will not be able to be crossed for the protection of the innocent and pure of heart.

Please hear this again, God is like a generator. His Energy sustains all planets and life forms everywhere. When God pulls back His Energy the impact of such a force will push the Godhead back and a gap will be created. This gap will exist in all times and all dimensions and all of those trapped on the other side, that were not pulled with the Godhead, will perish.

All of the Lightworkers are being asked to help free as many beings and planets as possible from the Evasion energy before God reverses His Energy. Many of the Lightworkers are working on other planets and in other dimensions at the same time as they are working on Earth. They are working to free up all beings everywhere who are willing to let go of this darkness.

The eye of Evasion envisions a reality exactly opposite of the reality envisioned through the Eye of God. God's perfect idea is to see energy flowing and creating in perfect balance and harmony, going out and coming in with freedom and beauty. Evasion's idea is exactly the opposite; worlds and universes with drone and robot-like beings. There is no creativity. There is no Light or beauty. A being's only purpose of existing is to work to feed Evasion.

Evasion is now invading planets and forcing them to relinquish their personal essence to it. Your Earth is in grave danger. The Earth feels she is being seized against her will. It is like a rape taking place that she is not willing to participate in, but because the consciousness of the beings on her are feeding this dark-source energy, it is entering into her. The Earth's original essence is pure and beautiful and loving, just like your own was in the beginning. Each time a planet is overtaken by this darkness an imbalance is created which affects all of the rest of creation.

THE CLINIC

ASHTAR speaks about the Clinic:

To this day there is still butchery going on aboard the dark starship called the Clinic. The number of beings who are being taken there has greatly increased because the dark forces have been intensifying their efforts. Many of you have blocked memories of the atrocities you either experienced or observed aboard the Clinic. Before leaving, you were psychically programmed to believe that nothing negative or unnatural happened to you so you could continue on in your normal third-dimensional reality. Yet, the impressions of what was done are registered in your etheric bodies.

Some of you actually worked aboard the Clinic in other times. Your hearts and your brains were removed and replaced by artificial organs that were programmed to keep your emotions at a low ebb to enable you to witness dramatic surgeries and to not think beyond the task that you were performing. For complete healing you need to remove the impressions from all of the devices and implants you received during these surgeries. These old impressions create blocks in your existing bodies. All of your stored memories from these times hold strong emotional charges, for you saw and experienced unbearable conditions.

Please understand that there are actual devices now present in human beings from current experimentation. Whether the device or implant is current or you are holding impressions from old ones, energy is blocked. If your energy is not flowing in a way that is natural, all of your bodies will be adversely effected -- the physical, the vital force, the emotional, the mental and the spiritual.

As I said, many people are being drawn to the Clinic or one of its scout ships because the dark forces are not finished with their work. They now have their plan perfected and can take someone aboard and within earth-time minutes return them with all of the implants in place which allow essence to be taken. Now it has become an exact science unlike the earlier stages when much of what you experienced centered around experiments of figuring out how to tap into and clone your life-force energy. Implants have been placed in humans to allow the dark forces to constantly siphon energy.

Many Lightworkers are unaware they have implants. Much of the powerful energies they bring through for healing others and the Earth is being siphoned from them by the dark forces, leaving the Lightworkers in a constantly depleted state. Many of these beautiful beings, who truly would like to stay on Earth and help, are asking to leave because they feel it is hopeless to continue on. Many have already left. They have been pulled back to a safe realm to heal, for they are connected to the Source.

There are also many who do not have a strong connection to the Source and the dark forces are literally draining them of all of their life-force energy. This is very serious, for when this happens it is as though their very souls are being sucked from them. Think of the soul as a spark of the God Source, a little generator that feeds all of the functions within your body. When this generator is actually sucked out, taken -- there is nothing left. The soul is gone.

Many newborn babies are still being experimented on. The dark forces are creating new races of beings in a most unnatural way. They are crossing the genetics of humans with the genetics of other alien forces to create a race that will be totally controlled by them. There are many of these beings already infiltrated into the human race. This has been going on for a long time.

We spoke to you before about looking into the eyes to know who is real and who is not. These cloned beings look like humans because of the crossing of genetics, and yet they are not. They do not have original God Essence flowing within them. They will attach and cord to a parent or a sibling and get fed essence in this way.

We know all of this seems like a bad fairy tale to you. The universal God Energy that is being sent to you now is holding this Truth within it. You must know Truth to free yourselves from the dark forces. Remember that what these forces are trying to create is a universe that will continually feed them and their dark source of energy, Evasion. We repeat, many cloned beings are on your Earth and are working very diligently for the dark forces. They are programmed to do whatever they are told and they do not feel any emotion. They are programmed to respond with normal human emotions, but they are not really experiencing the emotional energy that is common to those of true human form.

THE UNKNOWN OBSTACLE TO MANIFESTING

We spoke to you of the reflections that God gave to the Beings of Light to show the unlimited possibilities of creating, and also what could happen if Light is misused. No rules or limits were given along with these reflections and, as we reiterate, energy was given to images in the reflections and these images became vital. These images began to take over the essences that fed them, your own God Essences.

You must retrieve your lost essence from the beings that you created from these images. In the beginning they were just mirror images of what could be, of what could become of your Light essence if it was manipulated. You created many distorted pictures in your minds (reflections) and then energized them. These images took form and began to control the very energies that created them.

This was a great misuse of energy. Just because you have misused your power and energy in the past does not mean you cannot learn to use it now appropriately, but you must be willing to look at where you went wrong.

Many people are trying to teach how to manifest through mental imagery. They are teaching you to hold mental pictures of what you want to manifest and then connect up with the God Energy, the Source of All that says, "Yes, you can have whatever you want. You can create whatever you want." The process, itself, is not incorrect. Yet if you do not understand where you are distorting that process and correct it, you will never have true manifestation powers. It is frustrating because it cannot work.

You have to take back your energy from the now very powerful evil entities and energy fields, that you have created through your mental imagery, before you will be able to manifest correctly. Your ability to manifest will not shift until you free yourself from the dark forces. When you misused your God-given power to manifest, you took it out of alignment with the universal energetic pattern of how to manifest. You explored and experimented and took it out of alignment and now it is truly time to retrieve your lost essence and correct your alignment. You have to actually unhook from the dark forces, claim back your power and integrate it again within you. It will then be possible to connect back up in correct alignment with the Universal Energies.

AFFIRMATIONS

For God to be able to effectively work with me and help me, I must believe in Him again and let go of all dark force interferences.

I desire to be free from all dark force energies that have penetrated my being. Discarding these interferences frees me to return to my original essence, which is pure, beautiful and loving.

I retrieve all my lost essence so that I can once again be whole and complete and aligned with the God Energy. When I am truly aligned with God, all is possible; all can be achieved.

I will not allow my fears to hold me back. I call out strongly to the Beings of Light to assist me. I call on God Himself to come to my rescue. I believe in You, God. I will do my part. I claim back my essence and my power.

I am aligned with You, God. I am one with You. I am aligned with You and I exist for others to see that it is possible to be aligned with You.

It is possible to be joyful and to give and receive love. For God, You are love and I am love along with You. The power within me receives You now. The power within me releases all darkness now. The power within me will accept only Truth.

AFFIRMATIONS

I want to change. I want to learn. I want to be in balance and alignment with You, God and Your creation. I release my fear of unworthiness to receive the help I need to transform enough to be One with You, God.

Coming Home to God means going inward, to the very core of my existence, and finding the thread that holds me connected at all times to God's life-giving Energy. This thread of life leads me to the greater part of myself, my High Self, which knows Truth. I reconnect my mind to my High Self and again know Truth.

Total surrender is required to truly align and become One with God. I must surrender everything within me that is not of original God Essence.

I am a God-Being, created from original God Essence. I am God, therefore, I am worthy to be reunited with more of Myself. I reunite with my God Energy.

SIX

THE CONSPIRACY BEGINS

Long, long ago, many magical beings roamed your Earth plane in perfect harmony and contentment. One day a vast and mighty spacecraft appeared in the sky. Vast and mighty, we say, because it filled the sky farther than most could see. From this ship came the most haunting of music. It mesmerized all who heard it and drew them closer to the ship. Many beautiful, magical beings were drawn aboard by the music of this ship.

Once aboard they were scanned with the most amazing equipment. This equipment monitored every function within their bodies. All of their responses were monitored, even at the emotional level. They were individually charted and then taken to a treatment room where they received numerous devices and implants. Much examining and sample-taking of body parts was done in this treatment room. When all of this was completed they were returned to the Earth plane, to their beloved homeland, but they were changed forever.

Many of the beings drawn aboard this dark spacecraft were original soul essences who were experiencing a physical body for the first time. Because of their originality they were of extreme interest to the dark forces. They were innocent in nature, loving beings, free in their movements. They knew nothing of bondage until this music came, this mesmerizing music that drew them to this spaceship, and it is here that the torture and suffering all began.

For many lifetimes after, these original beings were continually abducted by this dark spaceship. They were constantly studied and monitored and experimented on. They did not know why this was being done to them. They did not even remember the experiences after they happened. They received strong programming after each experience that suggested they forget about what had happened to them. It felt safer to their minds not to remember.

The children of these beings were also taken to this dark spaceship. Sometimes the growing fetuses would disappear right from the wombs of their mothers, or the abductions would begin soon after birth. The child would be taken while the mother and father slept. Both of the parents would be kept unconscious and unaware as the result of an implant in their brain stems that would vibrate a certain frequency that literally turned them off. These frequencies would numb the brain from receiving input and stun the nervous system. It was a paralyzing which started with the implant in the brain and went throughout the entire nervous system. The parents would be unaware of what was going on and could not respond when the child was taken aboard this dark spaceship. The children were experimented on and many implants and monitoring systems were placed within them. This continued from generation to generation, and it still continues today, my children, it still continues today.

What was the draw? What drew these very beautiful beings aboard this dark spaceship for the first time? The music, the mesmerizing music. And why did it have such an effect on these beings? Because, my children, the very clever and cunning aspects of Lucifer knew how to recreate the sounds of creation and when these sounds touched the ears of those beautiful beings, they remembered and came forward voluntarily to investigate. They thought it was their God on this ship calling them to enter. It was a cunning ploy, my children, for it was not their God calling them, it was Lucifer, the god of darkness, the god of evil, the god of deception. Many aspects of his own cloned energy were aboard this ship.

You see, my children, Lucifer was very angry at your God, very angry. At one time he was accepted among you. He walked and talked among you and manifested as you did. This took place long before your Earth lives. Then he was noticed as not being quite right by the Beings of Light who were closest to the Source. They noticed there was something different about Lucifer. He looked like Light and behaved in a similar manner as the other Light Beings, yet something didn't seemed quite right.

Those that noticed this difference in Lucifer went and questioned the Father and Mother aspects of God. They said, "Do you remember conceiving this being that now calls himself Lucifer? Do you remember when he emerged out of You? We are not able to place him and yet he walks among us so confidently."

The Source of All had not paid that much attention to this being named Lucifer. He was busy, with the Mother aspect of Himself, creating more. He had not been keeping track of who and what emerged when; He just went on creating. This lent a new sense of responsibility and He answered, "Was I supposed to be watching and keeping track? I thought My role was just to create and to generate more and enjoy and revel in the beauty and ecstasy of it all." But because these beloved Beings of Light questioned that there was one among them that didn't seem to fit, He lent His Eye to this being named Lucifer, who pranced so proudly around the Godhead cleverly displaying his power.

As the Eye of God looked deeply into Lucifer, He saw the thread of untruth. Lucifer was not connected to Him in the same way as the other Light Beings. The vital force connection that came out of Him and went into all of His children was not there with Lucifer. Lucifer had a connection, but it was very hidden and came out behind him like a tail. This connection was Light but it was not attached to the God Source directly. As God followed this connection, that looked more like a tail, He found that it was hooked into other beings in the Godhead. So, in a sense, Lucifer was connected to Him and pulling essence from Him, but this was being done through others that He, the God Source, had created.

God was very taken aback about this finding and at first did not know how to react. He was very upset. He questioned, "What am I to do? How did this happen? What is this being named Lucifer? I don't have a clue what to do.

Should I just cut him loose and shake him off? But he is connected to all these other beings. Did they birth him? Where did he come from?"

He was truly confused and He consulted with the aspect of Himself called the Mother. She also did not remember birthing this being named Lucifer and when She looked She did not find Her divine connection to him either. She did see this tail coming out from behind him, hidden, yet definitely there, and saw that it was connected to others in the Godhead. She was also confused and discussed the situation with the Father aspect of God.

Meanwhile, Lucifer was planning a coup. He was planning to overtake the Godhead and he was hooking into as many of the beings surrounding the Godhead as possible. He did this by filling them with wrong ideas about power and glory. He would say, "You know, I think you could be much more powerful on your own. This God that you are so attached to limits your power. He is constantly watching over everything that you do. Doesn't that get old? Don't you get tired of that constant vigilance, knowing that every-thing you do is visible and that you can't hide anything from Him? He sees everything. Don't you get really tired of that? It gives me the creeps to think of being watched over in that manner. You know, I have a feeling that if you could just get out of His Energy you would feel much better and be more powerful. I see so much potential within you that you have not even tapped into. I see that, and I don't see Him allowing you to tap into more power. Do you know why? I think that if He saw what you were actually capable of doing He would be jealous. He is never going to allow you to have that kind of power. He will only let you do things that don't show Him up. That's pretty much the way it is, but you know, I think if we would combine our energies we could probably show Him a few things."

Many beings in the Godhead were very naive and Lucifer seemed especially attractive to them. They had already played in this reflection. The reason why Lucifer existed at all is because they gave energy to this reflection and now they were connected. They were still connected to the Source of All, but were also connected to this being named Lucifer. These naive Beings of Light really didn't see the hidden connection between themselves and Lucifer. They were drawn to Lucifer because he seemed very wise and appeared to care about them. They liked the attention he gave them. They would sit at his feet and listen to his plots and plans for long periods of time.

However, there were a few beings who were very loyal to the Godhead and felt it was their role to protect It right from the moment they emerged from the One. There was no conflict within these beings. It felt natural to them to want to protect the Godhead. One of these beings is known to you as Archangel Michael. Archangel Michael began to watch the way Lucifer interacted with the other Beings of Light. He was becoming more and more concerned by the undercurrent he felt coming from many of the beings in the Godhead. He felt their growing restlessness as they began to tug and pull away from the Godhead.

Archangel Michael felt it was his duty to keep creation flowing smoothly and rhythmically and in perfect balance. Now he definitely heard inharmonious tones. For you see, there is music with creation, beautiful music. One cannot create without the music from the Source. This music has resided within each and every one of you from the moment you emerged from the One. You hold within you the melody, the song of your own emergence from the One.

Archangel Michael went and told the Father and Mother that he suspected Lucifer was turning many beings against Them and that he believed Lucifer was planning to overtake the Godhead. God could not believe that this was possible, yet He also felt the unrest, the undertow of unhappiness that was feeding back to Him. This was a new experience. It created a feeling within Him of needing protection, a feeling that something was happening that would threaten the Mother, the Godhead and all of the beautiful beings who still flowed so smoothly in and out of His Energy.

God gave Archangel Michael permission to push Lucifer out of the God-head, because He could see that Lucifer was not created from Him. When Archangel Michael pushed on Lucifer with all his force, all of the other Beings of Light that were attached to Lucifer were also pushed. Archangel Michael was strongly connected to the Source and had an unlimited supply of energy to draw on. Lucifer, at this time, had only a group of beings to draw on, and they were confused when they felt this tremendous impact of Archangel

Michael's force. They did not resist because they were confused. They had no idea what was happening and why they were being pushed from the God-head. All they knew was to cling to this being named Lucifer. It was obvious to them that they were being pushed out of the Godhead and Lucifer was saying to them, "Come with me for safety."

They did not know that if they would have just severed and cut the connection that had formed so strongly between themselves and Lucifer, they could have easily been drawn back into the Godhead and into safety. But they did not know this. With tremendous force Archangel Michael pushed Lucifer far, far away from the Godhead, outside of the boundaries of creation. Remember, the God Source is constantly creating and expanding out, so it took a tremendous force of energy to push Lucifer outside the boundaries of creation into the nothingness. The group of Light Beings that were attached to Lucifer were pushed into the darkness as well.

The force of Archangel Michael's push was so mighty that it snapped the connection between the Beings of Light who were pushed with Lucifer and the God Source. When the Source of All felt this snap He suffered greatly and lamented over the loss of these beautiful creations of His Light. The Mother grieved along with Him. All of the beings in the Godhead grieved. No one, not even the Source, knew what had happened to the beloved beings who were pushed out to the outer edge of creation with Lucifer and into the darkness.

"Obviously they will all perish," was the rumored thought flowing among the Beings of Light, "They'll all perish, for how can one live without Light? They will all perish. They are gone."

The Source of All thought deeply upon this matter. He had created all of these beings and fed them constantly with His Light, and now that they were disconnected from His Light, it seemed only logical, only rational, that as soon as their own little generators, the sparks that were their souls, ran out of essence, they would no longer exist. He knew there wasn't much time to find these beings and bring them Home. He knew they could not survive very long in the darkness without His Light.

But yet, who could He send? Who would go into this darkness to retrieve these beings and how would they be found? There would be sparks of Light noticeable from their soul essence. They should be able to see the sparks flickering in the darkness, but they would have to hurry, and the darkness was so vast. The darkness was unknown. How could they find them in time and what about this being named Lucifer who had caused this problem? How were they supposed to deal with him in the darkness?

Councils were immediately formed and serious consultations began among all of the hierarchies in the Godhead. They came together and helped the Source choose the best plan of action. Archangel Michael brought a loyal and trusted team to the table and Ashtar did the same. For you see, Archangel Michael patrolled certain realms and Ashtar patrolled others. They worked together to keep all of creation flowing in harmony.

We know we digress here, but you need to understand what was going on in creation. For you see, the dimensions needed patrolling. The Rays of Light were developing individual traits and abilities and often organized competitions which frequently ended in spats. Archangel Michael, Ashtar and the beings that were dedicated to helping them, patrolled the dimensions and helped those in conflict sort out their differences. This was not done in a negative or judgmental way. There was never any threats of punishment given if beings did not behave in a certain manner. Peace was restored by bringing a harmonious vibration to the discord. This harmonious vibration helped those who had gotten out of alignment to see clearly and attuned them once again with the Source.

So, as Archangel Michael had his patrol, so did Ashtar, who sat at the right hand of God. Ashtar was very close to the Source of All. He was considered God's best confidant, his most valued counsel. At times this caused jealousy among the other manifested beings. At times, even the Mother Aspect of God wondered why the Source of All gave so much time and attention to this beloved being Ashtar. Yet She was very pleased to see such loving Light so close to the Godhead. It felt protective and so She allowed it. Archangel Michael was always pure in his intent and was never upset with petty jealousies, but many of the angels in his command felt competitive toward the different feeling vibrations of Ashtar and the Beings of Light in his command. Ashtar and Archangel Michael had only the highest respect for each other.

They knew they were working for the same cause, to keep peace and harmony throughout creation.

THE CREATION OF THE SHADOW SELF

The Beings of Light were all very busy creating. As creation grew it became more of a challenge to constantly patrol and keep the peace among the newly emerged beings who were not so experienced, and yet were given great power and as much energy as they wanted to experiment, explore and play with. And that is why, my dear children, the shadow self was created.

As was stated, Archangel Michael and Ashtar noticed how the newly created beings had a tendency to fight among each other and were becoming very mischievous, playing pranks on each other that often ended in heated debates. They were becoming very competitive. They noticed some of these beings were developing feelings of superiority. Those who were very confident of who they were did not have this problem, but the newly emerged beings who were coming about so quickly did not really understand where they had come from and what their existence was really about. All they knew is they existed and had great power, but they didn't have guidelines or rules explaining how to use it. Because of their lack of knowledge, they began to create knots in their energy fields. They quarreled with each other over petty things like who could leap the highest, who could run the fastest, and these little quarrels would create knots. It was like a war going on within their minds, but it was not meant to do any malice or harm. Their very new, undeveloped minds were exploring ways to use God's Energy and they used it against each other.

It became more and more of a challenge to keep up with all the disharmonies because the Source of All was very busy creating. Once the creative process began it did not stop. As creation grew it became challenging for Ashtar and Archangel Michael to keep up with it all. They had little time to revel at the feet of the Lord and languish in His Light, for now they were kept busy on patrol sorting out energy knots and difficulties. Not only did the young Beings of Light quarrel with each other, but they merged with each other and became all tangled up in each other. Sometimes it was an awful mess trying to figure out who was who, and who belonged where. Everything wasn't in its right place and it began to feel very chaotic in creation. The Beings of Light kept creating these tangles and knots that constantly needed to be combed out.

The untangling was done by bringing back the original vibration, the original sounds that the Light Beings were created with, and that would bring them back into alignment. "Oh yes," they would say, "Now I remember, okay, let go," and they would flow again smoothly. These sounds are very important. For you see, they are the seed sounds of creation. Different sounds are emitted with different emergences of beings. You were not all created with the same sound. It took a certain distinct sound to bring a group of beings back into alignment with their place in creation. We all have a place in creation.

Please understand that this was becoming a growing problem to the Godhead, so Archangel Michael, Ashtar, and a few of the other beloved beings that you know of today as the Ancient Ones, took counsel with the Source of All. They lamented, "What can we do? This is getting out of control. We are having no leisure time now. All we are doing is running around untangling these messes. We do love these younger Beings of Light, but what about us? Isn't there some way that we can give these beings checks and balances so they remember who they are and where they belong? It is really becoming difficult because they are merged in all over the place and it is taking us so long to sort them back out. Creation gets tangled at the edges and in between and we know You are aware of this, Father. We hear You burping and belching as You try to create and Your Energy gets constricted from these knots. Things are not flowing smoothly anymore and it is becoming too much work to untangle the messes."

God had to admit that it felt like He was having major heartburn most of the time that He and the Mother were together. He spoke to the Council before Him, "So that's what is going on. It used to be so easy to emerge new beings. My Energy used to flow so smoothly, and now I am having to use force. The Mother and I have not been looking out into creation. We have been busy just creating. So this is what's causing the problem. Well, okay, let's think about it."

Until a problem arose there wasn't any reason to think about it. As They pondered over the problem They said, "The beings are forgetting who they are and where they belong and they're becoming all mixed up and competitive. What if we give them a reminder, a blueprint of who they are? What if each blueprint is encoded with an imprint of who they are, so all they need to do is look within and see, 'Oh, okay, this is my form and this is where I belong. That makes perfect sense.'"

This is when, my children, the concept of the shadow self occurred. It was decided to give the created beings a shadow within them to remind them of who they were, an imprinted reflection to look at so they would always know how to get back into their original forms. This seemed like an excellent idea to all the members of the Council.

God said, "I will get busy and make sure that all created beings have within their make-up an imprint of their original coding. Then as they emerge, this imprint will also come forward as a constant reminder of who they are and where they belong." The Mother and the Father got together and worked out the details since it was within Them that this new coding needed to be created.

The Beings of Light were fascinated with their new shadows that went wherever they went and did whatever they did. For a while they were preoccupied with their shadows rather than with each other. After a while they became bored and that is when the mischief began. They decided,

"Okay, if you are my constant companion, let me try giving you some energy and see what we can do. Let me give you some energy to give you some life of your own. I am getting tired of just dragging you around without you doing anything."

They took their energy, which was in unlimited amounts from the Source, and added it to their shadows. The shadows became living entities. This was very fascinating and interesting to the Beings of Light. They merged with their shadows and explored many ways to play in them. Now that the shadows were vital, they were much more interesting. The shadow energies became very strong and soon began to take control of the Beings of Light who fed them each time they merged and played in them. The shadows were given to help the newly created Beings of Light, but they misunderstood the purpose and became entrapped by their own energy. They brought their shadows to life and then found they could not control them. (See Diagram 2)

Lucifer is truly not a being of God Essence. He was created by the manipulation of Light taken into the shadows of beings who chose to create with distorted reflections. Understand that some of the beings who were given shadows did not play in them. But some were mischievous and did. It was these beings who lost essence to their shadows each time they merged with them. The more they played in the shadow the more distorted it became. It did not look like their form anymore. Slowly the now distorted essence of these Light Beings began to take form within their shadows.

The first formed being out of the manipulated shadow essence was Lucifer. Lucifer actually emerged out of distorted energy of Beings of Light. He emerged as a separate entity and yet could not exist without constantly feeding off the energies of the Light Beings who created him.

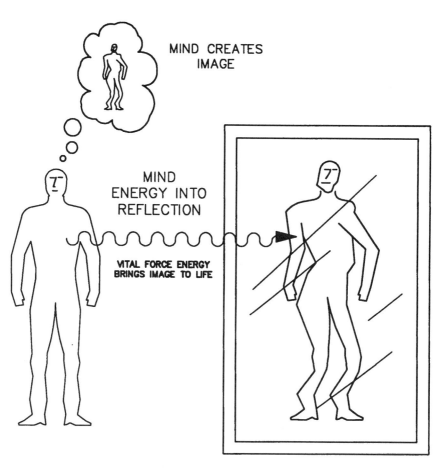

MIND CREATES
IMAGE

MIND
ENERGY INTO
REFLECTION

VITAL FORCE ENERGY
BRINGS IMAGE TO LIFE

DISTORTED REFLECTION

AFFIRMATIONS

I release all misunderstandings I have been fed about power and glory. God does not limit my power. When I am strongly aligned with the Source and in my full power I have an unlimited supply of God's Energy to draw on.

SEVEN

LUCIFER'S MASTER PLAN

Lucifer is your denial. You do not want to believe that he exists because of your participation in his creation. You merged with your shadows and then with each other. Lucifer is the result of your lack of understanding of how God's creative power is meant to be used.

Lucifer disguised himself in order to walk among you and be accepted. His master plan is to keep adding to his power source until it encompasses enough energy to overtake the Godhead. This was his plan from the beginning of his existence. Whenever Lucifer's inharmonious vibrations would be felt and the hierarchical patrols would search for the cause of the disturbance, Lucifer would band together the Light Beings he fed off and move them around. He played this game for quite awhile to buy time to get as much energy as possible before his coup was discovered.

The Light Beings enjoyed participating in Lucifer's game because he made them feel important and powerful. Each time he felt the approaching patrols he would say, "Oh look, here come the babysitters. They are coming to see if you are being good children or bad children. Don't you get tired of them constantly watching you? Come on, let's hide from them. Let's get out of here. We can't do anything without them checking it out to see if it meets with their approval. Aren't you wise enough to be on your own? Obviously this God, the Source of All, does not trust you at all. He sends out babysitters to see what you are doing because He doesn't trust that you can take care of yourselves. Come on, let's move around. Let's play hide and seek and show them a thing or two. Let's show them how cunning and wise you are. You know they think they are elite and your worth and power isn't as great as theirs."

With inflated egos the Beings of Light would agree. "Why should we have to be watched all of the time and told what to do and what not to do by these beings who think they are so special and important? Let's hide from them. That sounds like fun. Let's do it."

Lucifer was very cunning. He knew how to influence the Light Beings into believing that their God, their beautiful God of Goodness, was not there to help and protect them, but to hinder them from becoming all powerful. He relentlessly played upon this concept until great unrest grew in many of the Light Beings and they followed him and began to consider him their leader.

When Lucifer's coup was discovered by Archangel Michael and Ashtar, the Godhead was informed. The only solution seen was to remove the cause of all the unrest. Lucifer had to go. However, they did not realize the loss that this would create. No one knew that these beautiful Beings of Light would be pulled into the darkness with Lucifer. This is exactly what happened! We now return to the place in the story where there was much lamenting in the

Godhead, much lamenting over the loss of these beautiful souls.

A search party was organized. Only those in the strongest alignment with the Lord of All were chosen to go on this assignment. The assignment was to retrieve the lost souls before it was too late, before they would be lost forever. The Lord of All asked His most beloved and trusted Rays of Light to go out into the darkness and find these lost souls and bring them back to the God-head before their flickering Lights went out. He knew that without His Light feeding them they would not be able to sustain themselves, since their connection to Him was severed when Archangel Michael pushed Lucifer into the darkness.

There were no judgment feelings in the Godhead, only feelings of loss and sorrow over the separation of these beloved lost souls from the Source of their existence. Please understand that every Ray of Light, every created soul, has a place in the Godhead, and when that place is dormant there is a feeling of loss and sorrow. For, it is all of the individual Rays, the individual souls, that create the beauty and the flow of creation. When even one is lost it upsets the entire balance.

Beautiful Light ships were created for the search party to travel in. It took some doing but crafts of manifested Light were created to carry these chosen Rays through the different dimensions in search of the lost Rays. These Light vehicles were whirling disks of Light, powered by the God Source, that could easily traverse the different dimensions. God's chosen Beings of Light boarded these Light vehicles and went in search of the lost souls.

They searched and they searched and at times would catch a glimmer of Light, but before they could find it the Light would go out. They would think, "Too late. We are too late again." They would tirelessly search for long periods of time and then go back to the Godhead and report, "It feels hopeless, oh Lord, oh God of All, it feels hopeless, we cannot find the lost souls. They are nowhere to be seen. We catch glimpses of their Light and then it vanishes from our eyes. We feel that it is best to just forget this mission, Lord. It seems fruitless and hopeless."

But the Mother and Father Aspects of God could not forget. These lost souls were Their children. How could They forget when They continually experienced the loss? They were consumed with grief and Their only consolation was knowing something was being done to bring Their children Home. They sent out the Light ships again and again and said, "Search further, go further, they must be there. Go further, do not be afraid. We will sustain you. It is not hopeless. We can feel within Our hearts that they are still alive. They are still present somewhere out there. Please do not give up. We cannot abandon the Godhead and search Ourselves. We must keep generating energy to sustain all of creation. We cannot leave. We can only send out Our representatives, manifestations of Ourselves." Because the Beings of Light who made up the search party were so devoted and dedicated to the Godhead, they would return to their Light ships and continue to traverse the dimensions in search of the lost souls.

In the meantime, Lucifer had devised a plan. The Beings of Light who were pulled with Lucifer when he was pushed out of the boundaries of creation were frightened and they clung to him and lamented, "Help us! Help us please! You said you could help us and now we are lost. What can we do? We feel the Light of our souls becoming dimmer and dimmer. Soon we will no longer exist. Oh, help us! You said you could help us. Now help us!"

Lucifer knew that unless he could get more Light he was in great jeopardy. He would no longer exist once these souls he was feeding off were used up. He knew that he must devise a plan to survive. After some thoughtful deliberation Lucifer addressed the children sharply. "Children, children, come now, snap out of it! I have a plan. Now you know for sure that I was right about this God of yours. He certainly doesn't care for you. He just pushed you right out. He wanted you gone. We need to seek revenge. We need to take what is rightfully ours, the Godhead. The control of the Godhead should be yours, my children. All of creation belongs to you. It was never His. It belongs to you and you must take it. I can help you. I have a plan, but you must follow my every command."

The children were very torn because they remembered how it felt to be with their God. It was such a pure, loving, accepting, gentle flow of energy. What Lucifer was presenting to them felt dark and cold and domineering. Yet, they felt they had no choice since they could not feel God's Energy anymore. They felt they had no choice but to align with Lucifer completely. They did so with heavy hearts burdened with guilt. They forlornly thought to themselves, "If only I would not have played in my shadow, if only ... now it

109

is too late. God has cast me out. I have no choice but to align with Lucifer. I can feel my Light becoming dimmer and dimmer. I have no choice."

Lucifer devised a plan. He then instructed the children, "We must carefully sneak back to the boundaries of creation and take what we want by force. We must plunder and we must rape. We need to be very clever to avoid the patrol that is always searching and watching. We need to create a vehicle to traverse the different dimensions and it must look like the ones created by your God. Children, do you remember what those vehicles looked like? Do you remember what music they played? Come on, come on, out with it, you know. It's all within you. I can see it there. I can read the impressions. All you have to do is let me have your essence which holds the knowledge I need, and before you know it we will have created our own light vehicle."

The children really did not want to give this up. It felt like giving up the very blueprint of who they were. Yet they were so desperate they allowed Lucifer to take whatever he needed. This had been his plan all along. He had carefully plotted and planned which Light Beings to trick and get to follow him because he needed the essence they held for his master conspiracy to recreate the Godhead and to become more powerful than the Godhead.

He planned to hold the Godhead and all the Beings of Light subservient to his newly-created godhead. Remember, Lucifer and his creations cannot exist without Light. There was no way to figure out how to recreate the generator Itself, the God Essence that creates. His plan had to be to constantly get Light from those who fed from the Godhead. He carefully accumulated a group of beings who had all of the information in their essence from every emergence, from every burst of life that came forth from the Godhead. From these essences he learned enough to recreate a universe, for his master plan, that looks similar to the one created by the God of Light and Goodness. Lucifer's created universe looks similar, yet it has no Light of its own. It is merely a shadow of God's creation. It is merely a reflection of God's Light.

Lucifer is very cunning. He has figured out how to duplicate everything within God's creation. He has created exact duplicates by taking essence and Light from different beings. When it came time to create a light vehicle he had all the necessary information that he took from the beings that held this knowledge. With his keen scrutiny he was able to read the music within each of these beings that came forth from the Godhead when they were created. Each Being of Light had this music within. Lucifer could read the vibrations, identify the frequency of the music and put a melody to it. He busily tested and analyzed all of the Light Beings. He took their patterns of music from them and distorted this music to have a mesmerizing effect on those who resonated to the same sounds. Time was of the essence. The lights of the souls that Lucifer now held captive were becoming dimmer and he needed more Light soon to maintain his own existence.

Lucifer quickly created a light vehicle and manned it with those Beings of Light that were now totally in his control. He had done this by taking out their God-created music, the vibration that made them respond to the God

Source, and placed inside of them his own vibration and frequency. This Luciferian frequency made these Beings of Light feel that Lucifer was truly their creator. Without their God-created melody, the pulsing life-force they had emerged with, they could not even vaguely remember or feel anything within them that reminded them of the Godhead. They manned the light vehicle as robots, still alive from the spark of God Energy of their souls, yet totally controlled by Lucifer's vibration. Like robots responding to a central control unit, they followed Lucifer's every command. They were directed to go to all the different planets in God's creation where the other beautiful Beings of Light dwelled. Lucifer's master computer was programmed with information about the beings on each of the planets. He now knew which melodies they had emerged with. He gained all of this knowledge by taking it from the Beings of Light he held captive when he scanned them for information. Each Light Being had deep within his original coding the entire scheme of God's creation.

Lucifer's light vehicle first approached planet Earth at the time you know of as Atlantis. He began to play the melody, the sound of creation, that the beautiful Beings of Light who dwelled there resonated to. They were drawn to the light vehicle like magnets. The mesmerizing sound confused them and they thought it was God's Light vehicle calling them. They thought it was perhaps just a routine check-in with Archangel Michael or Ashtar, since they regularly patrolled all of creation. Many Light Beings were drawn to Lucifer's spaceship. The horror that followed is what we need to speak of next.

ZIKIA, MASTER SURGEON OF THE CLINIC

One of the beings that traveled on Lucifer's light vehicle was a master surgeon we know of today as Zikia. Zikia was capable of performing the most intricate of surgeries on the bodies of the Light Beings taken aboard Lucifer's spaceship, which we will now call the Clinic. Zikia was programmed, and his computer-like mind was fed all of the input needed to experiment on every aspect of existence. He was to come up with a program that would fit the master plan of his creator, Lucifer. The immediate focus was to get essence from abducted Beings of Light, since the original beings that were in Lucifer's control were almost used up. Lucifer's command to Zikia and his drones was at first, "Take the essence! Get it in any way you can. We will work on refining this later, but now we need Light, we need essence. Be careful not to kill these beings. We have to find a way to hook into them so we can constantly feed off them without them becoming aware of what we are doing. We will have to do something to their brains. We have to program them so they don't know what we've done. This is very important because if they remember they will go crying to their Creator and our plan will be ruined."

At first, very gross devices were placed inside the bodies of these Light Beings who were abducted on different planets. We say different planets because your planet was not the only one that was being preyed upon at this time. Very gross devices that would constantly draw essence out of the beings they were placed in were created very quickly by Zikia, the master surgeon.

Lucifer and his cohorts could now take essence from the beings that held devices whenever they needed to, which was often. They also placed monitoring devices inside the Light Beings so they could study the responses and results of their experimentation at all levels -- physical, emotional, mental and spiritual. They observed that the life span of the bodies of the Light Beings carrying these devices became short. Lucifer decreed, "We have to make sure that these Light Beings keep reproducing and as they reproduce we must find ways to immediately hook into the new creations. We have to make sure that this happens so we will continue to have more and more essence to work with."

Some beings were kept on the Clinic as breeders. These beings were restrained like laboratory animals and bred to produce for Lucifer's experiments. Many of the Light Beings were returned back to their home planets. Lucifer was wise enough not to keep them all. He needed programmed Light Beings on the planets to accomplish his goal. Taking essence from the people and the planets enabled him to create his own universe with his own planets. Lucifer knew he would need to create lifelines from the God-created beings and planets to his own created beings and planets in order to sustain his universe.

Lucifer was very careful not to disrupt too much at one time. It had to look as if things were still okay and in balance. He knew that if he removed all of the beings on a planet Archangel Michael, Ashtar and the other guardians who came around on patrol would become concerned since it wasn't common for a whole group of people to leave their home planet. Yes, many came and went in the spirit of exploring and sharing with others from other places, but a core group was always left behind to hold the energy patterns of the original inhabitants. Therefore, many abducted Light Beings were programmed and sent back to their beloved lands. When the patrols came through everything looked as if it was going smoothly and the patrols would continue on their very busy schedules.

The beings on the Clinic were duplicated many times. Many clones were created to increase the manpower. Lucifer needed massive manpower to build his envisioned empire. Light Beings were dissected and some of their organs were placed within these clones in a way that would not cut off the vital force of the Light Being from flowing to its original organ. Artificial organs that were created by Zikia, the master surgeon Lucifer programmed so well, were skillfully placed in the Light Beings to replace their stolen organs.

Zikia was brilliant and his skills became more advanced and sophisticated. He was like a machine, a computer, and the more input he was given the more cunning ways he created to take essence and literally build beings. Even though organ parts were taken, many of the Light Beings were kept alive because the artificial organs placed within them kept their vital energy flowing, even though it was programmed now to be sent to the organs that had been taken out and put into the clones. Remember, these clones have no life-force energy of their own. They are not connected to the God Source, they must be fed life-force energy by someone who is a God-created being.

Lucifer's master plan became more elaborate. He created a space station out in the nothingness, his own inner city manned with beings who are totally in his control. Lucifer and his cohorts built many crafts and spaceships that would traverse the inner planes and the outer dimensions in search of more essence and more materials for his creations. He has taken samples from every species and every planet, many yet unknown to you, and he has recreated God's creations. All of Lucifer's creations take energy from God's creations and pass it through their vehicles to sustain them. Then it is taken from them by the massive energy source that we know of today as Evasion.

Evasion is the master energy source that Lucifer created from all of the essence taken from the Light Beings. Evasion is like a power plant that changes God-created essence as it is taken, and stores it until Lucifer and his hierarchy want to use it. All formed dark energies come out of this source, Evasion. All of the beings who are created by Lucifer or have fallen prey to his plan are like drones. They have no power of their own. They obey instructions and perform whatever duties they are programmed to do and then give over whatever they collect and gather to their maker. Lucifer is truly their maker, their creator. Lucifer's beings do not carry within them the God Song, the sounds of creation. Instead they carry the vibration of Lucifer.

EIGHT

GOD'S SOLUTIONS

GOD speaks:

My beloved children, please listen to these grave tidings. Many of you are about to perish unless you heed My warning and return to My protection, to My Light. I am about to intervene with Lucifer's master plan. I am going to withdraw My Light. By withdrawing My Light, I will cut off the energy flow that feeds Lucifer and his creations. Now children, understand that when I do this, those who are not connected to Me will be lost. When I pull back, I will pull back with full force and this reversal of the flow of My Energy will cause such an impact that a gap will be created. All the planets are now resonating to the impulses I am sending to prepare them for this happening. Only those of you who are aligned with Me and can move with My Energy will be saved. If only I could convey to you the tremendous risk I am about to take by reversing the flow of My Energy. I know I will lose many of you, and yet if I do not do this I will lose you all and eventually Myself. There is little time left, My children. The Luciferian forces are pulling on Me. I must release them soon and allow them to dissipate in the darkness.

This will be a time of excruciating pain for those of the Light who are not

117

directly connected to Me and are left in the Luciferian darkness. Without My flow of Energy, those now so hungry for essence will begin feeding like vultures. When there is no Light essence left, they will turn on their own kind and consume each other.

I have been sending out signals for some time now for all of you to awaken and reconnect so I may gently guide you back into alignment. But there are so many impediments interfering with you effectively receiving My messages. You are being kept unaware of what is truly going on. You have so much fear you are not even listening. You are busily running here and there, creating this and that, even though none of your activity brings you any real happiness or fulfillment.

Children, heed My words. Soon your Earth will begin erupting as a last attempt to awaken you from your slumber. And so it is with a heavy heart that I deliver these words to you. I have great love for all of you. Each soul lost will be grieved and the places you held within Me will remain empty for all the days to come.

The ANCIENT HIERARCHY speaks:

Many beings are uniting against the spirit of the new age. We speak of the new age as the age of transformation, the age of removing all darkness and returning to the Light. That is the only definition we give for the new age, the age of returning to the Light. Many of you have been trapped in the darkness for so long that you have forgotten how it feels to be connected to the Light.

Your High Self is aligned with God's Light. Your lower self, the ego, is constantly thinking it is in charge and ignores the guidance and wisdom available through communication with your High Self. It is the lower nature of man that gets caught up and then manipulated by the dark forces.

Your High Self cannot be disconnected from the Source. This is the part of you that is always within the Source of All. This is your God Self. Think of a sun to symbolize the Source of All, a big burning ball of Light. Within the make-up of this tremendous ball of Light there are many, many particles which represent your High Selves. From these High Selves, Rays of Light go out and the souls of man are at the end of the Rays. Your soul is a spark of God at the end of the Ray and all of your bodies are formed around it. Your High Self cannot be taken from the Source. It is secure within the Godhead. Your High Self is a seed of God from which you were created and from which you emerged. The little spark at the other end of the Ray, the soul, the home of the God Essence within the man, can definitely be taken.

If the connection between the High Self and the soul is severed, the manifestation around the soul spark will die unless it is fed from someplace else. The only other place to be fed is from someone who is still connected to the Source. You need to understand how all of this works because there are many beings who have separated from their High Selves and stay alive by feeding off others. These beings who feed off others do it for their own survival. They either have forgotten how to connect to the Source or they have no interest because to do so would mean they would have to change their ways and follow God's Plan for man.

God has told you of His Plan to ensure the safety of your soul essence. In order for His Plan to work your soul must be connected to its High Self. God needs to be released from the heavy burden of the parasitic darkness that is feeding off Him through you. To assist His release, it is vitally important that you let go of your connections to the dark forces. God does not want to pull any dark energy into the safety zone He is going to create. If you have not released yourself from the dark energies there will be a tug of war when God pulls back His Light. There are many souls connected to the dark energies. It will take a tremendous force of God Energy just to pull Himself away. Those of you who are connected to your High Selves, but have not cleared your own darkness, are still in danger. If the dark energies have a strong hold within you, when God pulls back His Light, you could be severed from your High Self. Please understand this. You can no longer ignore the reality of what is truly happening on your planet. If you are still being controlled by the dark forces, which work against God's Plan for man, at the time God reverses His flow of Energy your soul may be lost. Without your soul you will not be able to manifest again. You will no longer exist.

When God pulls back His Light, a gap will be created between the darkness and the Light. The darkness will not be able to cross this gap because a strong field of energy will be created that cannot be penetrated by either side. The darkness will be trapped on one side and the Light will be on the other side. For a period of time rebuilding of all the basic structures of God's creation will occur. There won't be much expansion until all of the planets and the beings of Light have achieved balance.

You do not have to be totally healed and in balance to be saved. You must be connected to your High Self and freed from the dark energies. We encourage you now to seek out the Lightworkers who can help you with this process. Ask with sincerity to be guided to those who have developed the spiritual abilities and healing modalities to help you. Many skilled practitioners are ready to assist you. These Lightworkers have already aligned with God's Energy and have freed themselves from the dark, dense energies. They are also capable of assisting you in awakening your God-given abilities and personal soul mission.

After the pulling away, there will be time for total healing. All of your energy bodies will be healed and attuned to the Universal God Energy. You will be taught the basic Universal Laws of manifesting and co-existing. The healing process will be quick because there will not be any darkness left to interfere and trick you into holding onto your illusions. It will just be a matter of releasing whatever is not in alignment with God's Light and attuning to His Energy and Will.

Very magical, beautiful Centers of Healing and Light will be built to assist all who are seeking help. The vibrations of the structures themselves will elicit spontaneous releases and realignment with the Source of All. These beautiful Healing Temples will also help heal and realign the Earth and bring her back into perfect balance and power.

While this restorative and healing period is going on for all the planets and the people who have survived the great changes, all of the souls who have been trapped on the other side of the gap will be devoured by the dark energy force we call Evasion. When there is nothing left to feed on, Evasion will not be able to continue its existence and will dissolve and dissipate into nothingness.

Then, when the time of danger has passed, God will push against the protective energy field until it breaks and creation will begin anew. Think about a mother's womb as she is creating and nurturing a child and the protection of the uterus. The amniotic sac and the fluids keep the child in its own protected environment while it develops. That is what it will be like as we rebuild. First there will be the period of healing and development within, and when it is time and the protection is not necessary, it will be broken and expansion will begin. And then, totally aligned with the Source of All, living in harmony and in balance with your Earth Mother, you will once again be able to manifest everything you need and desire. Fear, lack and limitation, unhappiness and unfulfillment will no longer be a part of your existence.

Sananda, Lord Jesus, would like to speak with you. So many of you are familiar with his energy and that is why he has been chosen to help you now. You trust his vibration because you have experienced it before. The Christ Energy is being made available to everyone who is sincerely seeking alignment with God. It will help to protect your soul and will assist you in becoming a Christ-like Being. Listen to Sananda's inspirational words and know that you are all capable of doing the exact same things he did during his lifetime as Jesus of Nazareth.

SANANDA speaks:

I am a joy vibration. When I was in human form I got caught up in the same things that you do. Many of you do not know the true story of what I went through. Do you know that I worked with the Light vehicles? I worked with the Light vehicles from a very early age. What an exciting experience that was! I was not afraid. It was so incredibly joyful. I received visions as a child. I had a very hard time relating to people around me because I saw energy patterns in everyone and everything. I would sit for hours, fascinated, as I studied my surroundings. My mother would say to me, "Why can't you play like the rest of the children? Don't be so noticeably different."

Yet my Mother and I were in close alignment. We both had human urges, but we also shared a strong will to do what we were sent to do. We knew we had purpose. We never forgot. We accomplished our missions because we were willing to be guided, in whatever form it came to us.

Much of my training was given to me on the Light vehicles. The beautiful Beings on the Light vehicles would come and pick me up at night when my Mother was sleeping. I would wait for them to call and then I'd slip away quietly. I would go outside and a beautiful beam of Light would encase me and lift me. I want to share this with you because many of you will experience this in your lifetime. This lifting is a beautiful feeling. It's exhilarating. It's joyful. The Beings I speak of are not the beings who are creating havoc on your Earth plane. They also have vehicles, but they are not Light Beings. When you are protected and aware, you can feel the difference. Light energy feels like love and joy. Dark energy feels like fear and confusion.

At the time I was on Earth the dark energy did not have as strong a hold as it does now. My mission was to create an opening to bring in the vibration of energy that was needed to help people spiritually evolve. Now we are bringing in a much higher vibration of energy. You must purify your vehicles to be able to carry this high vibration.

My energy is now so expanded that I can be in many physical forms at the same time. I can create many Rays. There is no one person that I favor. "Oh you, you are the chosen one." No. Who wants it? What I am saying is my energy is available to anyone who wants it, but you must be in your personal power to utilize it effectively.

Many of you are afraid to claim your power because of all the abuse of power and manipulation you have experienced. The dark forces have convinced you that you are powerless, that it is impossible to create and manifest as I demonstrated during my lifetime as Jesus. Don't be afraid to align with my energy and let me help you remember your own God-given abilities. My energy cannot be manipulated in any way. You cannot use it to harm another. What you can use it for is to create whatever you want and need that is in alignment with God's Plan and will work toward your Highest good.

Many atrocious acts of violence are being committed on your Earth plane. You can't even allow your children to walk to the corner alone without worrying that someone will do them harm. Is this the kind of Earth plane you want? It is not what we want. We want you to be happy again, to be able to create and to live in harmony, but you must be willing to do your part to assist us in helping you. You must work diligently to connect again to your High Self. You must clear all of your dark energies and claim back your power and awaken to your true nature. All it takes is intent and focus. It is time to make your spiritual development a priority in your life. We will teach those of you who are willing to prepare your vehicles how to manifest. After the Earth changes it will be a lot more comfortable for you if you know how to create what you need.

Some of you are meant to teach others this knowledge. You are meant to go into areas where people are living in fear and survival and say, "Relax. I am here to help you, relax. I can help. I am connected. I know how to manifest. Look, here comes a beautiful spaceship. Say hello, you are not alone. You weren't left here. Thank you for staying and now let's start rebuilding." This is going to happen. This is not going to be a sad time. It will be a time of great joy. All of the dark interfering energies will have been removed. You will have a fresh start. Doesn't that sound interesting? The only sadness is for the souls that will be lost, those that couldn't move with God's Light.

How many of you would like to keep your bodies youthful and vital? You can do that. It is possible. You have bought into the belief system of death and dying. You can keep your body but you must learn to master it. You don't need to allow disease. It is a belief system you have been fed. You have been fed lies. Immortality is possible for all.

Now, my Mother would like to say a few words. You should always honor your mothers for they gave you an opportunity. So many of you are in conflict with your mothers. You say, "Mother, you were a bad mother." This may be true, but did not that mother give you the opportunity to experience and grow? When I was on Earth my Mother felt very discounted. She felt, "I gave this child birth and he was literally taken from me. I was thanked for my contribution and then discounted." It was hard for her to accept so much, and yet she was willing.

MOTHER MARY speaks:

My children, please open now to my energy and I will help you heal your wounded hearts. You have closed your hearts in an effort to protect yourselves from experiencing more pain and disappointment. You must now open to experience God's Love, a love that is pure and everlasting, complete and fulfilling. You will need to trust in God's Love for you during this next trying period. I can hold you and give you comfort whenever you are in trauma over the changes that are coming to you. I am here for you but you must ask for my help. I can make you feel, "Oh, it's okay. I am loved. I am secure. Mother is here." How many children want their mothers when they are in need? "I want my mother. I want someone who will hold me and let me know it's going to be okay." You may not have a physical mother who is capable of doing this for you, but I am available. I volunteered for the job.

Whenever you need the security of being loved, call on me and allow me to comfort you. If you would allow me to work with you, you can also give out my energy to others who need love. You cannot possibly mother everyone, but you can give my energy to those who cannot reach it for themselves. You can give my energy to a room full of children that you are teaching, who are all in trauma because all of their parents are in trauma. You can wrap each one in a beautiful pink blanket of energy and they will feel, "Oh, we're okay. We are loved." You can do this with your best friend. This is so needed. Everyone needs love, from the strongest, most out-going person, to the most timid.

It is now time to activate God's Plan to help you. It is also time for you to take responsibility for your part in God's Plan. This is not a game. It is not a story. It is reality. We know how you struggle to keep up with the realities you have created. We understand it's hard for you to focus on spiritual growth when you are kept busy trying to pay your bills and take care of your children.

I am asking you to reach out to each other, to band together and support each other so you don't feel alone with your struggles. Help each other hold the spirit of positive change. We will support you, but you also need support from each other.

ASHTAR speaks:

Do not struggle. Let go of your struggles. There is no need to hold on to them. Understand that you only need to be willing and allow, allow. We will not misguide you. We will lead you down the correct road. Many of you are not seeing the road, but you know where God's Energy is pulling you. You know what you need to do, you feel it. You can trust your feelings as long as your intent is pure. We will always show you when you are off track. Attune to God's Energy and let It direct you, because as long as you are flowing with the Divine Current you will be safe. Get in, let go and flow. But as you are flowing, if you are holding on to something or someone along the way, you are going to get hurt. Look around you and within you and see what is keeping you from flowing. It may be a loved one. It may be a job. It may be that you are in the wrong location for what you need to do.

Did you know that your energy has been assigned to certain areas on Earth, places where you can channel through more energy because your vibration fits those areas? You don't have to stay in these areas all the time, but spending periods of time in these places will help you come into your own power. Where is God's Energy asking you to be? What is God's Energy asking you to do? It's not about being irresponsible. It's about being aligned with God's Energy and being in your power so that you are capable of fulfilling what is being asked of you. It is almost as if the Divine Current is a giant magnet and you are being moved around. This is necessary because you often do not make the changes that are important to your spiritual growth

128

because of your fears and attachments.

It is now time for fast movement. Much activity is needed and very quick uprooting is often necessary to be in the right place at the right time to help a certain group of people, or to connect with those that can help support you. Ask in Spirit, "Where is my support?" Then go where it is, and trust. This is important. Work on releasing all of your doubts, fears and insecurities, and when you feel solid within, move forward. Your confidence and your personal power will build with each successful change. There is always an uncomfortable transitional period while one is letting go of the old and grasping for the new. I am telling you that to reach the new you are going to have to let go of everything and everyone that is holding you back. So, look at those areas in your life, and then call on us for assistance. We will be there for comfort, for support, and for guidance. All the help you need has already been put in place. It is up to you now to reach out and accept this help. The hand of God is ready to grasp you securely and support you through this process.

AFFIRMATIONS

I return to God's protection and Light.

I am aligned with God's Light. I seek the guidance and wisdom that is available to me through communication with my High Self.

I awaken my God-given abilities and personal soul mission.

I release whatever I hold that is not in alignment with God's Light and attune to His Energy and Will.

I am willing to do my part to assist Spirit in helping me. My intent and focus is on diligently working to connect to my High Self, clearing all dark energies, claiming back my power and awakening to my true nature.

I make my spiritual development a priority in my life.

I open to Mother Mary's energy and ask her to help me heal my wounded heart so that I can open to experience God's pure and everlasting love. I renew my trust in God's love for me.

I ask Mother Mary to hold and comfort me whenever I am in trauma. I work to reach Mother Mary's energy and give it out to others who need love.

I take responsibility for my part in God's Plan and focus on my spiritual growth.

AFFIRMATIONS

I reach out to others of like mind. We band together for support and to help each other hold the spirit of positive change.

I let go of all struggle. I attune to God's Energy and feel where It is directing me. As long as I am flowing with the Divine Current I will be safe. I let go of everything that is keeping me from flowing.

I let go of my fears and attachments and make the changes that are important to my spiritual growth.

Spirit is here to assist me, to comfort me, to support me and to guide me. I reach out and accept this help.

SECTION II

INSPIRATIONAL MESSAGES

From The Source, Sananda, Mother Mary,
Archangel Michael, Ashtar and the Earth Mother

Waking Up

To Your Soul's Purpose

ADRIENE:

I will begin by bringing in the Christa Energy for all of you. To receive it you must open up your hearts. The Christa Energy is wake-up energy. When you open to this energy, it immediately wraps around your soul to protect it and then begins to vibrate your soul to a new level of awakening.

Those of you who can see colors will notice that this energy is the color of an emerald – a beautiful emerald green. Watch as it comes into me and out of my heart and into each one of you. It will fill you with what you need for this evening and vibrate all those little spots within you that are holding onto doubts, fears and indecisions. It will shake them loose in a very gentle, loving way.

You are here with purpose. The Cosmic Christ Energy that is here in this form, is to remind you of that purpose. It is here to help you manifest that purpose. It is here to be received and given out to others. It is here to be shared with everyone who is searching and seeking and crying out for help.

Ashtar wants to speak first this evening. Ashtar is a beloved being that sits close to the Godhead. He has been around since the very beginning of creation and has observed everything that has gone on, so he is very qualified to help implement the changes we need to make. God has placed Ashtar in charge of our Rescue Mission because he is so loyal and trusted.

The very evolved Beings that are coming to help us are pure in intent, and because of this purity, they will never interfere with our Free Will choices. They will not help us move from a stuck spot unless that is truly what we are seeking. Compassion is allowing for whatever our soul asks. That was the promise given to us in the very beginning and it is still the promise today. All of the high vibrational Light Beings will not assist you unless you ask. You have to want their help.

ASHTAR speaks:

People of the Earth, we have been assisting you from afar. We are helping you to find your right place in creation. It is now time to return creation to its original blueprint, back to its harmonious pattern of flow. Much information has been given about what is causing the interferences that are holding creation in a stuck place. I am using simplistic terms. I always use simplistic terms.

We have surrounded creation with a new vibration. This vibration is being activated by Light Beings in Spirit who are working on the Rescue Mission. Our forms are different than your forms. They are not as dense as your forms and they are easier to maintain. We are asking beings on the planets involved to allow us to channel this new vibration through them into their planets to ground it.

We are going to pull creation away from the energies that are holding it stuck. This has been explained as the Evasion energy, an energy that holds tight and is not allowing expansion. It is draining and pulling at the Earth Mother and other planets in your solar system and has a hold on the souls that inhabit these planets.

The Rescue Mission is to free up the planets and the beings on the planets, and to pull them back into the safety of the Light, the Light of the Godhead. This is the Rescue Mission. Many of you on Earth also dwell on other planets and are working in other dimensions. You are not limited in what you are capable of doing. Some of your essence is being held in your physical body. Many of you have agreed to take on the denseness of this physical vibration to assist the freeing up of trapped souls.

But what has happened, my dear children, is that you have forgotten what you came here to do. Many of you are aware that you have a role to play, but the memory of what your role is has been hidden deep within. There are ways to activate it. The ways are coming quickly now because soon God's Master Plan will be activated.

We do not want to activate the Master Plan until you are willing to receive and ground the energy to make this shift happen. The new form energy is coming into those who are already awake and allowing the vibration to come in through them, so there is shifting happening, but we need many more volunteers or we will not have enough grounding of energy to allow the planets to move with the vibration. It won't work. The energy will just slide over the surface. There is a tight shell of formed energy around your Earth

Mother that is preventing us from being able to directly send this energy to her.

There is an inner connectedness between your physicalness that is on the Earth and your other dimensional aspects, we will call them, which are connected to your High Self, which is part of the Godhead. Because of this connectedness, we can send this new vibration to those parts of you that are free and clear and not caught up in the Earth energy vibration, and you can send it down your channels and into your physicalness, and into the Earth. You must be willing to open yourselves up to more of who you are. This isn't anything unusual that is being asked of you. This is something that is built into who you already are. Many of the therapies that are coming into being at this time are to help open your channels. When you open your channels new information comes in from your other dimensional aspects.

You can always trust the information that comes from your own energy, especially if you pass it through the discernment of your High Self. It is also important that you strive to connect with your other dimensional aspects. When you connect with only your High Self, you are bypassing different parts of you which have been put in place to create dynamics that hold entire systems in balance. Think about physics and the things that you know about atoms and molecules and how they interrelate. You must activate all of your energy to create the wholeness needed to keep your systems functioning in a harmonious and balanced way. The Luciferian Conspiracy was explained to you in very simplistic terms, yet more scientific information could be given. It is important for you to understand that the breakdown of your structures began within each and every one of you.

Many of your therapies are designed to reactivate your original DNA structures that will reconnect you to your wholeness. You must first remove the distortions that caused your DNA to mutate from God's original coding.

SANANDA speaks:

My energy is similar to the lightest laughter you have ever experienced. Think of the moments when you laugh, it just flows out of you. It releases every tension in your body. There is no holding on. That is the energy I am bringing you this evening. As my energy comes into many of you, I feel you thinking, "Don't let this happen." Please, let it happen and experience my joy. I am true joy consciousness.

There is so much doom and gloom talk. As you say, "Not that doom and gloom stuff." You are not aware of the celebration that we have waiting for you after you move out of the tight hold of the dark energies and back into a dimension where you can receive us again freely.

Do not be afraid of the coming changes. It is going to feel so blissful. Why are you afraid to experience bliss again? You will be completely accepted for who you are. Can you imagine what that will feel like? The tension within you will release when you know that you are accepted wherever you go and by whomever you meet. You will be acknowledged by a sparkle in the eyes. You will get so, you know the term you use, so high. I hear your logical, practical minds thinking "How can we do anything if we are always walking around high? How can we accomplish our tasks?" Why do you want to have tasks? When creation is again flowing in harmony there will be no need for tasks as you know them.

Yes, there is going to be a transition period. It is not just going to change from extreme stuck to extreme bliss. I want you to experience some bliss so that you will know what you are working for. Struggle does not exist in the blissful state. After the transitional period only harmonious vibrations will exist.

When you look around and feel into what is happening in your world today, you easily observe the extreme imbalance of energies and know that walking around with a big grin on your face is not going to do much to change things. I am speaking of the promise of the new age. You are working to reach this promise. What is happening now is not the new age. You look around and say, "Where is all the joy? Where is all the bliss? Where is all this leading?" You are now transitioning out of the old consciousness of pain, fear, survival and powerlessness, and if you tune in at this level, you know there is going to be a lot of devastation and loss of life. There is fear of the whole concept of the new age because this is the first consciousness that you will run into. This layer does exist.

The hard shell of held energy around the Earth must be broken and removed to reach the dimension where harmony and balance can be restored. The tension of the energy force needed to successfully complete this transitioning is building. You feel the tension within yourself as well. All of your old structures are under stress as the new is coming in. You feel the strain of the new pushing against your deeply ingrained patterns of being and you think, "I don't dare bring in more energy or I am going to explode." Every system needs to expand to break through this tight hold.

As Ashtar stated, you are being asked to open to the new energies and channel them to your Earth Mother. As the new form energy builds, you will literally burst out of your old form shells. You can perceive this expansion as a rebirthing. The Earth also has to go through this process. She has to break out of her old form and expand. To expand, much of the formed energy that makes up her surfaces will change. It's a natural process.

Think about a child playing with a mold in the sand. The child packs the mold with sand and then puts it down and lifts the mold off carefully. When the mold comes off, it is easy to change the configuration of the sand, where before when it was in the mold, the sand was stuck in a set pattern. The molded energy around the Earth has to be lifted up and then the formed energy underneath will be able to shift and change to fit the new vibration.

MOTHER MARY speaks:

I am here to assist with softening the intense vibrations of change and upheaval. My energy feels soft and yet there is strength and an ability to protect within it. Some of you are delicate in nature and will have a difficult time withstanding the intense vibrations that are needed to break down all of the old systems. Call on me for assistance and my energy will soften your experiences and add soothing energetic support.

We watch the patterns of thoughts as they swirl around the Earth. There is a battle going on between beings that say, "Why are you trying to soften things? Don't soften it, let's just do it," and beings that send a softening energy every time there is some kind of disaster. The vibration is going to continue to build to such an intensity that unless there is some softening many beings will not be able to tolerate the feeling. My energy takes the edge off harsh situations making them more tolerable. This is important because if life becomes unbearable, you will choose to leave.

Openings have to be created for energies to come through the solid mass of held energy around the Earth. Many different types of energy are needed to assist your successful transition. One energy is not better than the other. All of the energies we are sending you synergistically work together. They all need to be channeled to the Earth to get the job done. Different beings will resonate with different energies. Some people will carry more than one energy which helps integrate the different energies. This means opening up and accepting what you are here to do. Each one of you should be striving to bring forth your own unique way of participating in God's Plan.

All of the energies are constantly changing and evolving. Each energy is coded with many different layers of vibrations, and each layer has a specific intent. Attune to the vibrational layers that you can now reach and work diligently to reach higher and higher frequencies.

SANANDA speaks:

Imagine what it feels like to be held in the arms of a loving mother for the very first time. All of you have had this experience in some incarnation. Feel the shear ecstasy of the experience.

When you were within your mother there was an understanding about how your systems were interrelated. You were being nurtured within her and you felt safe and secure. Then one day your world changed, with a tremendous contracting feeling pushing against you, you were expelled out of your mother. The fear of that experience is what most of you remember. You panicked, "I don't feel her." But then remember when she picked you up and drew you to her breast. As she cradled you, tears of joy streamed from her eyes, for she was so happy to see you outside of herself for the very first time. She did not wonder about the personality you would develop or worry about the belief systems you would take on as you grew. Your mother experienced only happiness and contentment in those first few moments of your life and her love vibrated into you. You felt her familiar energy and connected with her in a new way. You realized she hadn't abandoned you. Her loving arms were supporting you, her warm breast was nurturing you, again you felt safe and secure.

Your Earth Mother will deliver the final message for this evening. Your Earth Mother is a conscious being of formed energy -- very ancient and very wise. She has been so neglected. I feel deeply for the Earth Mother. She is my Mother also, for I have walked on her surfaces and I have served her and she has served me.

Many of you feel shameful for neglecting your Earth Mother. She has given and she has given, and she has always allowed you freedom to do as you choose. She has been so abused and now she is truly suffering.

Do you know that the dysfunctional family structures that are so prevalent within your societies originated from the abuse of the Mother? This is not intended to cause guilt and shame. Many are saying, "Let's change these patterns of abuse." How can you change something on the surface that has not yet changed inside at the core? The Mother is now ready to shift these core patterns that are causing herself and her children to suffer. I am explaining this so you will understand that what is about to occur is not punishment. What is about to occur is because of the love of the Mother for her children. It is because of that love.

The EARTH MOTHER speaks:

I love you so deeply. You are a part of me. I do not want to hurt you or cause you pain. But what I see is that you are all suffering and I am suffering along with you. I want the suffering to stop.

Your physical bodies are manifestations of the relationship we have when you come and dwell with me. It is as though there is an invisible umbilical cord between us which feeds nurturing energy back and forth. Most of you have forgotten this concept. You are to nurture me and I am to nurture you. In this way it is enjoyable for both of us.

Notice what is happening in your family structure. The mothers give and give and the children do not give back to them. They don't even realize that it is theirs to do. The mothers say, "That's okay, I love you anyway," because they do. But there is a disconnect that has happened which is keeping this flow from occurring and nurturing back to the mother.

I am not receiving love. I am empty and it is very painful. I am tired of being alone and not thought of as you trod along caught up in your own self-importance, "My gosh, it's my mother's birthday. What an inconvenience. Now I have to do something about it. What shall I do?" When you were young your mother's birthdays were very important. "How can I surprise her? How can I bring her joy?" As you grew and got more into your busyness your attitude became, "Oh, it's mother's birthday, I have to do something," and you felt guilt and shame about what was not done.

The reason your attitude shifted is because you lost touch with me, your Earth Mother. When you lost touch with me, you lost touch with all mother consciousness. Every mother can identify with my feelings of being used and abused by their children. Mothers feel the greatest gratification from the newborn child. They feel the infant's appreciation, "You are my world, you are my existence. I love you!" Whenever an infant sees its mother, it beams to her, "Oh, I love you. I love you. I love you." The baby never gets tired of beaming smiles of love and appreciation to its mother, and this feeds the mother and she feels full again. The mothers never say, "I am so sick of that child smiling at me. I wish he would just stop it."

When you were an infant, the mother was all there was, and that was enough. But as you grew and began to expand your consciousness, you touched other thought forms. The more you grew, the more you naturally touched all the structures that had already been put in place. It wasn't that you were wrong to touch these structures. You touched them because they were already there. These structures were formed by many minds who came before you. Many beings who came before you abused their energy and power and created systems that use your consciousness for their own fulfillment. It was not your fault. They planted the seeds of dysfunction in the structures for their own profit. This goes back to the very beginning. Energy was distorted and you fell into it because it exists. You touched it because it was there.

Some of you have gotten over the stumbling blocks of the child. You have gone through the growing pains and understand the importance of giving, and you do it. But you are blocking receiving. You are blocking receiving because of the guilt and shame you hold from your past actions that you now know were wrong. I am telling you that it is okay. I am not holding this against you. You can best help me by letting go of all your guilt and shame and feelings of unworthiness, and by allowing the higher energies to flow within you and into me. Then I will again be nurtured and feel full.

There are many ways of releasing old pain. Many therapies and methods have been created to help release the shame and guilt of the past in a non-judgmental manner, in a gentle celebration. "Yeah, it's over. You did it!"

146

Waking Up To Your Soul's Purpose

Your guilt, your shame and your old pain is like a tight corset. It is tight on you. If you would release it you could expand again. Remember that expansion is what is needed now. We are going to expand. You have got to release your corsets, your old blocked energies. As each person lets their blocks go there will be a sigh of relief. Some of the pain is gone.

I am encouraging you to release your pain and I am going to help you by releasing mine. I have long held pain and I must release it now. I cannot hold it any longer. I don't want to hold it any longer. I am going to release it soon and as it releases you are going to hear the groans within me. You are going to feel the shifting. It will sound like a mother giving birth as I let loose and release my pain. My process will frighten you if you don't understand why this shifting is occurring.

But if you understand what is waiting at the other end of those groans, you will encourage me. You will be like my coach saying, "Come on, Mother, you can do it. I am going to give you a little energy here to assist. You can do this, Mom! Come on, you can do it!" That will give me strength to do more. The more encouragement that I hear, in the form of energy sent to me, the more I will do and the easier it will be for me. If you make me do this alone and you do not help me, I am going to hurt myself in the process.

God's Energy has surrounded me to assist me in my rebirthing. It has created what looks like a sling over a weakened limb to provide me with extra support for this period. I want to heal and I need help healing. I cannot do it alone. I truly cannot. I need your assistance also and am asking that you remember and honor who I am and help me.

If I do my releasing with only the energy forces that are now in place, I will need emergency treatment. If we cooperatively work together, I can release my pain in stages. I am going to need a strong foundation to hold me through this period. I am going to need you to be like pillars saying, "Mother, we are here. We are sending energy to you. We are holding it down. We can do this."

Transformation will occur in everyone who stays and assists me. You will experience a tremendous shift in consciousness. We will vibrate and change together. You will not always feel well. I feel nauseous most of the time as I release all the old energy that needs to go, and you will feel nauseous as you assist and go through the same process. I hear people saying, "I don't know why my body hurts. I didn't do anything. What is going on?" Your discomfort is being caused by the changes that are occurring within you. Don't panic, hold on to the thought of the joy that we will experience when we are through with this transition.

I will survive this experience in one form or another, but what a shame to have to shatter myself into particles, when I could just transform if we work together. Much of how this process is done depends on your participation. There are many souls crying out, "But I don't know how to assist. I don't know how. Why am I not being shown what to do? Why am I not being shown what my part is? I'm just going to continue on in my ordinary way until somebody shows me."

It is time for the way-showers to come forward. Many of you are way-showers. You will vibrate an energy frequency and then a whole group of others will remember what they can do. "I can do that. I can help with that. That's good." Many sincere, loving souls are waiting to do their pieces and don't know the way. It is your piece to show them the way. You all know what is vibrating up within your souls. Don't be afraid to act on it.

You are awakening in waves. The first wave of awakening is that of the way-showers, those who are supposed to show the second wave the way. If the first wave does not awaken, how will the second wave awaken and how will the second wave awaken the third wave? You can get in touch with God's Plan for you. Connect with your High Self and ask, "What is my role and how does it fit into God's Plan?"

AFFIRMATIONS

I ask to remember what my role involves. I ask to be shown how to activate the memory, hidden deep within me, of what I came to Earth to do.

I am willing to open myself up to more of who I am. I align with the other dimensional aspects of myself which are connected to my High Self and are free and clear of the earth energy vibration. The new vibrational energies can then flow through my higher aspects, down my channels, into my physical vehicle and then into Mother Earth.

I remove the distortions that have caused my DNA to mutate from God's original coding. I reactivate the original DNA structure within me which will reconnect me to my wholeness. I return my DNA structure back to what it was in the beginning when all was flowing in perfect balance and harmony.

I remember to call upon Mother Mary often for help to cope with the intense vibrations around me. I ask you, Mother Mary, to take the edge off the harshness I feel, so that I have the strength to stay and help during the coming times.

I release all the pain, guilt, shame and feelings of unworthiness that I hold from my past actions which block me from receiving. I now open to receive freely. I open to receive and allow the higher energies to flow through me and into Mother Earth.

AFFIRMATIONS

I open up to and accept what I came to Earth to do. I now bring forth my own unique way of participating in God's Plan.

I willingly help Mother Earth through her transitional period and rebirth, for I remember and honor who she is.

I ask to be in touch with God's Plan for me. I connect with my High Self and ask to be shown what my role is and how it fits into God's Plan.

STAYING INSPIRED & CENTERED
DURING THESE CHANGING TIMES

ASHTAR speaks:

Welcome, we are happy to join you this evening. The veils are getting thinner, and when the barriers are broken we will be able to be with you and walk with you as One. Can you imagine what that will feel like, for us to be united again together as One? Oh, the celebration we have planned for you!

Ascension is near dear ones. Ascension is near. Without you ascension is not possible for the many. We are asking you to open to and ground the energy that makes ascension possible for many. You also have the ability within you to emanate energy out to others. Emanating energy to others is one of the most important things you can do to assist God's Plan. We have imprinted the energy we are asking you to bring through with the ascension plan.

Many of you have been receiving information about the ascension plan and know that this is definitely your piece. Now, I am asking you to open to the energy that will make your piece potent. Reflect on this for just a moment. In all of your sacred religions everything was empowered and made potent by Spirit. The mantras are empowered by the Masters, then passed on to the adept who passes them on to the student. This is how it worked in the past. It still works this way, except now we are asking you all to become masters. We are asking you to pass on your contribution, but pass it on empowered so it will work for others. When you have empowered your contribution for others they need not go through all the rigorous training that you have gone through to get to the same place. It can be quite simple. You can empower an entire room of people if their openness, willingness and sincerity is strong.

We are at a point in which very strong focus and very fast action are needed, but in a very balanced way. This does not mean running around frantically. This means focusing your energy like a laser, knowing exactly what to do, how to get it done and sticking true to your course.

Like vibrations attract like vibrations; this Universal Law has not shifted. When you bring through empowered energy, it will emanate out and attract the right people to you. Then when you go into a room the people who are there will be those who can truly receive from you. You will also draw in the connections who will help you move like the wind to accomplish your goals.

We are asking you to get going quickly now. The whole world is waiting, clamoring. You may have good business skills and be able to assist many people in that avenue. Don't think that the work is only about the spiritual healing modalities, it's about business and education and politics -- it's about all of this! Strong leaders are needed in all arenas to emanate out the correct way to do things, even the correct way to use power. There is so much abuse of power going on in your world. How to use power in a balanced way is something foreign to the people of the Earth, for there has been such a long period of imbalance.

The energy we are asking you to share with others vibrates, "This is how to use power without manipulation. This is how to live in balance and in harmony. This is how to work together and not harm each other."

MOTHER MARY speaks:

It is let-down time. Think about the relief of letting go. A nursing mother experiences this when her breasts are full of milk and the child begins to suckle, tension builds and builds and then it releases. This is the time we are approaching on your Earth plane, a time of releasing and letting go. I feel fear vibrating up within you about what the Earth will be going through.

Whenever Earth changes are mentioned everyone becomes tense. Think about letting go, letting go. To be a powerful facilitator of healing on your planet you must be able to remain in a relaxed state. This is challenging, so challenging, and yet know this is needed.

You must first achieve the ability to stay strong and relaxed in your personal lives, and then together we can emanate strength and balance to the world. Know that the situation is under control. It may not look controlled, but it is! There will be massive panic and hysteria beyond anything you can imagine as the Earth begins to shift and change. We are asking you to emanate out a vibration which will say to the world, "It is okay. The situation is under control." This is going to be so important.

As soon as the first major Earth shiftings occur, and this shifting is close at hand, large groups of people will be seeking help. People will be hungry for help at all levels. Strong leaders are needed in every walk of life and field of endeavor to emanate out to others, "You can have your life in control." Teach your methods and share your knowledge, but also emanate this energy because so many will be frightened. Intense fear will attract more harm and disruption. Exemplify a balanced state of mind that is confident of finding solutions to every problem.

This is a time when those who are aware are asking, "Where should we live? Where should we move? Where are the safe places on Earth?" You must learn to hold the consciousness of balance and harmony to make wherever you choose to live a safe place. You will need the assistance of several strong spiritual beings to hold an area stable. This can be done while the rest of the Earth shifts around you.

Wherever you are being drawn is where you need to be to assist those who are in that area. Trust that the God Energy will not disappoint you and will not let you down. You will be safe. This is our solemn promise to all who follow their Guidance and work for the highest good of all. You will be safe, whether you are in an inner city or out on a coastline. Take in this understanding and let go of your fear, because everyone is feeling the readiness of Mother Earth to shift and change.

You must learn to extend your energy and reach out further and further. You have the ability to hold energy fields. The held energy field is what makes an area safe. Those who vibrate to anger and fear will gravitate to where there is more anger and fear, because like attracts like. Some of you live this concept in a positive way and have easily moved through life never fearing bodily harm coming to you. You do not emanate negative vibrations and therefore do not attract them to you. This is an important concept to teach to others. Everyone must learn how to clear their negative vibrations and return to balance.

Communities are needed, even small group communities that are not totally self-sufficient. Some will be in cities. A community is a group of like-minded people who are working for the same cause and support each other. Your community may be three or four people, or it may be larger. The important factor is to have enough physical vehicles to hold an energy field around your physical space. This is very important.

Those who travel out to help others will need to travel with a support system of five to seven people. This will help us guarantee your protection. You are here to help us. We love you. We honor you. We will do whatever we can to protect you and to make your work come to fruition. You will need to travel out in groups, little caravans. Being with people who you trust and who energize you will bring you joy as you do your work. You will be joyful! Even in the chaos and the distress that you will see and feel, you will be able to generate a bountiful amount of joy energy and emanate this positive vibration to others. Those who you reach will respond, "My, you have something. You have something and it feels wonderful! With all of this going on you're not in fear and survival." And they will come and listen to you, because what they are responding to is your vibration. That is what interests people in what you have to offer, your vibration.

ARCHANGEL MICHAEL speaks:

I am here to remind you to play! I noticed how heavy your energy became when we spoke of the serious situations and that is why I am asking you to keep your vibration high and remember to take time to play. Play with each other. Dance with each other. Create celebrations that are truly celebrations. When was the last time you had a gathering that truly was a celebration, when you went out of your minds with ecstasy and you let go of control? It feels wonderful. This is what we want to see going on in your communities. We want to see this openness of energy, this joyful expression of your spirits.

You are the Green Berets, here to do a tough job that only a few have signed up for. Some who did sign up are not participating. Green Berets deserting their posts, can you imagine? Oh, we are going to talk with them when they come back! They are going to be most embarrassed and they will lose their wings for awhile. This will be done gently and without judgment. Before you are accepted into the Green Berets, you are tested and we are assured that you will do the pieces that we assign you. Some people are hiding their Green Beret hats so they are not identified.

Relax and be joyful. "We will do the best we can with what we have!" "We will do the best we can with what we have." This will have to be your motto to get you through these changing times. It sounds a little silly, but know that we are supporting you. You must do the best you can with what you have! Emanate this vibration out to others to help those who will have so little to hold onto.

You have so many roles to play at so many levels, but you are capable. We tested you – remember? We tested you, "Can you bring through joy?" Yes, yes. "Can you bring through balance?" Yes, yes. "Can you get past all the distortions and illusions on the Earth plane?" Uh, oh. Some of you did not test all the way positive with this one, but we decided to send you on assignment anyway. We told you, "Do the best with what you have," because we had so few volunteers who even wanted to try. The scoldings won't be too harsh, because we understand that you are being asked to stretch and stretch and stretch. You are all walking around on Earth like taut rubber bands. You are already so tense it wouldn't take much more to send you flying out of your bodies. What about the rest of the people that you came to help?

We are asking you to help at so many levels that some of you are getting confused about your missions. You are working in the physical realm as well as the other dimensions and then you get distracted with, "Oh, wait a minute, I have to make lunch for my children," or you remember that the laundry needs to be done. We understand your challenges. We understand, and what is going to get you through this extreme tension and help you survive is dance, dancing with your energy in whatever way your energy enjoys dancing. What brings joy to you?

You also need playmates! Dancing alone has its merits, but dancing with someone else always brings more joy. We have been urging you to join with

159

others of like vibration, so you can create a bountiful flow of energy. Most spiritual beings are lonely beings. We hear them lamenting, "We are dedicated, but we are lonely." You need playmates. Imagine the spirals of energy that will be created when you are with people who vibrate at a similar frequency. Much more can be sent through even two people who are vibrationally compatible, for shifting consciousness or for anything else that you are trying to achieve.

There will soon be a mass exodus off your planet. There is preparation going on in the realms of Spirit to receive and make the way safe for all of those who are planning to leave. It is not so easy to leave anymore. You must be able to find the openings that will take you through the density around the Earth and in the upper dimensions. It is just not an easy out. You cannot get from the Earth plane to the Spirit realms without going through what has been created. This needs to be understood. We are busy working on openings to assist the large numbers of people who will die in the earthquakes and the other catastrophic events that are coming up. We are going to try our best to make sure everyone has a safe crossing.

We need your help in opening these portals, we'll call them, and in assisting others with their crossings. Uh, oh, you've got those serious looks again! See how quickly your energy gets heavy when the subject goes back to death and dying?

There will be some lifting-off of beings in physical bodies during the big devastational shake-up. Those who are lifted off will return later to help with the rebuilding. It is spaceships that will lift you off the Earth and spaceships that will bring you back. There are certain areas that will be opened for this lifting-off of physical bodies. Those of you who are choosing this alternative will need to hone your awareness to make sure you are guided to the right place at the right time.

You have all been talking about ascension. There is ascension happening all the time, but at different levels. What I am talking about now is physically lifting off the beings that want to maintain their physical vehicles and then come back with them. This is important, because there will be so much work to be done.

It is important to have information given to you that will touch and trigger those parts in you that need activating. As long as you are aligned with your Guidance you will know where to go and what to do. There will be no waiting, you must be on time! This evacuation has been planned since the very beginning of the Rescue Mission.

Evacuation is at hand. Evacuation and ascension go hand-in-hand. Those who are able and want to ascend will ascend. Those who are able and want to stay will stay. The rest of the Earth's inhabitants are going to be evacuated one way or another.

AFFIRMATIONS

I focus my mental energy like a laser, knowing exactly what to do, how to do it, and I stay true to my course.

The Universal Law is "like attracts like." When I bring through empowered energy it emanates out and attracts to me the right people who can truly receive from me. I draw in the connections who will help me move like the wind to accomplish my goals.

No matter how much panic and hysteria there is around me, I will remain confident and emanate to others that God has the situation under control and they can also have control in their lives.

I will share my knowledge and methods of staying balanced with others who are seeking help. I will be an example of a balanced state of mind that is confident of finding solutions to every problem.

I ask to be guided to live where I need to be in order to be of assistance in that area. I trust that the God Energy will protect me.

Spirit loves me. I am here to help Spirit. They will do whatever they can to protect me and make my work come to fruition.

State Of Affairs
On Earth Today

SANANDA speaks:

I ask you to open your hearts and receive me. I am here to help you absorb everything that is said and surround you with strength and peacefulness. If you stay and help your Earth Mother weather out the storm, she is going to reward you by helping you do all the wonderful miraculous things you were meant to do while living on her surface. She has stored much wisdom that she has not been able to release to you. So many of you have been looking only to Spirit for this wisdom. Some of you know that the Earth holds wisdom, but you have not been able to receive the real gifts that are at her core. After the Earth changes, these gifts will flow out to all those who can receive. You might request, "Mother, all of my water supply is contaminated. Please show me how to purify it." You must integrate the knowledge you receive from Spirit with your Mother's wisdom to unlock the secrets of manifesting.

You helped create your Earth Mother. There is much written about the theory of evolution, how your planet was formed and how the people of your planet came into existence. Did they evolve, or did they come from other places, or did they overshadow and merge with ancient animals? There is so much confusion because all of this happened, it's not one or the other. There are so many scenarios that have taken place on your Earth. Many of you helped create your Earth Mother when you were in Spirit. You did this by drawing on the beautiful God Energy and focusing It through your very powerful minds.

Think of the Godhead as beautiful pulsating Light Energy. It feels warm and blissful as It flows through you. And then you have a thought, "I would like a drink of cool, clear water," and the water manifests. This is possible. In the beginning of your existence there was no separation between you and the beautiful God Energy. You knew you were a part of God's Energy and yet you were given the gift to create with individual expression. You were not given a set of rules that said, "Think this and don't think that." Now you have so many limiting beliefs and thought forms encasing you that you can't even remember what it felt like when you created with ease.

You all did not come out of the Source at the same time, there were many different emergences of Light. Those of you who emerged at the same time often created together. These beings are considered to be your spiritual family and are the most comforting for you to be around because they have a similar vibrational make-up.

We are asking you to draw members of your spiritual family near to you now. They are usually not in the families you were born into. More often you meet these beings in the workplace or through group gatherings or by taking a trip across the world. It is so magical how you connect, but remember the Law of your Universe is "like attracts like." Send your vibration out with strong intent in a wave of energy. People on the other side of the world, the other side of the city or the other side of the room will connect with your vibration and then you will be drawn together. Your High Selves will arrange the meetings. It is so easy. It happens all the time and you say, "What a coincidence. I met the most incredible person at the zoo. I was just standing by the monkeys." Was that a coincidence? No.

So many of you are lonely. I hear you lament, "I love you Jesus, but frankly, you can't accompany me to a movie. It's hard to share a meal with you and really get into the physical aspects of it." If I chose to be in physical form I would enjoy a meal with you! One of my greatest memories is of well prepared food. You have pleasures on your planet that are to be enjoyed. After the Earth changes you will have only simple pleasures to satisfy you. So many of the luxuries that you are accustomed to will not be available for quite some time. I suggest you draw in someone who likes to cook even if their vibration does not quite fit yours!

Being surrounded with your spiritual family will trigger you to remember how to create with others. You will easily learn to read each other's thoughts. It happens naturally between people of like vibration because it's so easy to attune to energy that is similar to your own. There is great potential for harmony when you are all in alignment and focused on common community goals.

You have the ability to do so much. You can have one lovely large family that you have birthed through yourself. Some of you have the most incredible children, they are teardrops of joy. Think about the times that you have been so emotionally touched that your eyes well up with tears. Some of your children carry exquisite joy vibrations, and yet they are troubled because they are feeling disharmony. Many of them feel unsafe and vulnerable because their parents do not know how to protect them. Some of these beautiful children are crying out to go Home to the Godhead. These children are not just the ones who are young in years, they are of all ages.

ADRIENE:

Mother Mary is overshadowing me now and I feel her powerful emotion. Often you hear that the Hierarchy does not display any emotions. They have very evolved emotional bodies. They still feel strong compassion and love, but they have evolved their emotional bodies past the lower nature emotions that many of us become entrapped in.

MOTHER MARY speaks:

After the first big Earth release many of your blinders will be removed. These blinders are energetic patterns that have been holding you from seeing with your physical eyes what is going on around you. When this release happens you are going to be shocked at what you see. When you are able to see Truth through your physical eyes you will be moved to help. Most of you are going to want to run, "Ahhh, I can't stay here. This is awful. I work for someone who doesn't even have a soul. I can't go back to the office." What are you going to do, take a gun and shoot them? That would be a wrong action. You must hold your balance and your peacefulness. With your blinders removed, the Lightworkers will also be more visible and you can confidently seek out employment or association with those who are strongly aligned with God's Light.

Many of you are busy visualizing new ways to live and yet unless you release all of your distortions, these new ways will not manifest. I experienced these distortions when I lived on your Earth plane. I know how difficult it is to work through them. You are fortunate because there are now ways and means to help you remove all the interferences that are keeping your positive thoughts and visions from manifesting. There are healers who understand. There are scientists who have created wonderful God-given instruments that can actually transmute distorted energies. Your governments are not wanting to bring this technology forward. Your governments want to hold you in illusion because then you are easier to control. "But we're electing them," you are saying. How much power do the people you elect really have? I am telling you they have very little power because these are not the beings who are truly controlling your planet. Your elected officials are mere puppet heads. They keep very busy. They form committees to create change and yet they truly do not have the power to make decisions.

Your governments are being controlled by a world organization made up of very powerful beings who have come from different environments. There will be much outbreak of war between nations. This is a situation that is not at all under control, for this world organization decides which governments to upset to get what they want. You are being played for fools, everything is being orchestrated. Some of the Earth changes that will occur will not be in alignment with our Plan to assist the Earth. This controlling group of beings have very powerful plans to disturb certain areas of the Earth. No amount of bandage energy is going to alter their plans because these beings do not resonate to the frequency of love and Light. You cannot shift them.

Many of you are under the illusion that you can transform dark negative energies by sending them love and Light. This does not work because these dark beings have no love and Light within them. They are manipulated essences, which means they were created from God Essence taken from Light Beings and changed to an energy that does not respond to love and Light. These manipulated essences do not respond to God. Who do they respond to? They respond to Lucifer. They respond to Lucifer and the large group of beings that he works through and controls. This is very serious information. Resonate with my heart and know that I am speaking about these matters because I care so much for all of you.

For some time now you have been experiencing germ warfare on your planet. There are germs that have been deliberately created and directed to certain areas of the Earth. Yet, there is a way to be free of all of the vibrations that distort into illnesses. Remember that everything is vibration, everything. If you resonate to disease energy you will attract disease energy to you. If you release your distortions and positively charge your energy, nothing can harm you. I am not suggesting you drink water contaminated with diseases. Please do not challenge yourself in this way. I am urging you to use every possible method known to purify and positively charge the food you eat and the water you drink.

But also know that if you did drink disease-laden water, you could remove the disease vibration. "Oh, wait a minute, this is not what I want." You are powerful beings, you can do this, but you have to remove your vulnerabilities. You are programmed to believe that diseases are contagious. "Oh, please don't sneeze on me because if you sneeze on me I'm going to catch your cold. Don't do it! Now you did it, now I've got it." You have so many layers of impressions that vibrate to this belief, even though you say, "Yes, I'm strong." If somebody sneezes, you loose it.

Many mothers know the secret of immunity. When their children are sick they affirm, "I have to take care of my children, but I'm not taking on their illness." Are you instructing your children correctly? How do you respond when they come home from school and say, "Mommy, daddy, five of my friends broke out in chicken pox." Do you say, "Oh, you're going to get chicken pox next." Or do you say with confidence, "When that disease energy comes toward you, don't take it in." You have to teach them correctly. And if your child has already picked up some of the disease energy, you can draw it out of his body. You must release all of your fears and limiting belief systems. You don't have to be a victim to your environment.

California is experiencing much pain and fear because it is about to erupt with the greatest earthquake it has ever known. There is much energy work being done in the area by well-meaning Lightworkers who are trying to prevent this eruption from happening. It is well-meaning and yet it is not going to be effective for much longer, because the Plan must move forward. We are not happy about the loss of life and the pain that will occur, but yet the time has come for your Earth Mother to be released from her suffering. You think you are helping her by holding her old form in place. "Mother, let me help you. I know you are in pain. Let me put this soft bandage on you. Don't explode Mother, don't erupt."

You know how uncomfortable it is when you are incredibly sick inside and someone tells you, "Don't throw up. Hold it in." Your Mother is full of poison and is getting sicker and sicker. If she holds it in, she will become seriously damaged at her core. We will not allow that to happen.

You must be willing to flow with the Earth changes. Develop a positive attitude, "Do you like it when the Earth moves? I like it. It feels powerful to me. It feels empowering and it feels right. I'm not afraid."

The EARTH MOTHER speaks:

My preparation stage is over. What was solidly held within me is now loose enough to begin to release. I am grateful that this stage is over and yet I am afraid to continue my process. I know you understand the fear that comes when it is time to give birth. There is excitement in the anticipation. There is the extreme agony of the labor, and when it comes to the birth -- there is fear.

I must now release my fear and hold onto the vision of what is waiting for me.

I am literally birthing myself out. I feel like an empty shell that has been used up, abused and no longer in a form that I even like. Yes, I still have some beauty. You see it in the mountains, you see it in the forest, but you do not see it in your everyday life. I now want to support a world where all will walk in beauty and joy.

I am having last-minute anxiety and worry. I'm not sure I can do this because I am birthing something new. I am getting reassurance from my coaches in Spirit, but I also need your support. I am asking you to help me through this process. You are my closest connection. I can touch and feel you. I want you right beside me saying, "Mother it's okay, do it. It's okay, we're right here. We're right here." Can you do that for me? I have sacrificed myself for your experience many times.

I know that once I begin to release I will not be able to stop until the entire process has been completed. All of you mothers have experienced this feeling while giving birth. Once you've begun the birthing process there is no turning back no matter how uncomfortable you become. And when the labor and birthing is done, the celebrating begins.

But what is going to happen to all of you who do not go through this birthing process with me? Understand that as I am releasing my old form energy and birthing my new energetic pattern, you must also go through the same process. You will still have a physical form as I will still have a physical form. But what is going to happen to those of you who do not shed your old restricted patterns? Some of you will have the good fortune to get off my surface and be assisted to places in other dimensions, or on other planets. You will have opportunity to experience what you need for your growth in another place.

But there are many, many beautiful souls who will be lost in the transition. I know your minds wonder, "How can that be?" If you are not connected to the God Source you will not have a safe transition. Those who are not connected to the God Source are getting their energy to function from others. Many of you are attached to people who you are keeping alive with your own energy because you are fearful of losing them. This is not the way to help your loved ones. You must detach from them so they realize they need to connect to and get nourishment from the God Source.

The process is really not that difficult. You must unhook from all of the dark energies that are holding you. This tug-of-war between the dark energies and the Light energies is also happening within me. The dark energies have wrapped around my core. God has decided to intervene now to help me get free of the dark source that holds me stuck. All of you who are not aligned with God and are still connected with this dark source will not be freed with me. You will be pulled into the darkness and no one will be able to rescue you because it won't be safe to do so.

I am going to do whatever it takes to free myself so I can begin to recreate an environment that will serve you. I want to be able to assist you in manifesting and creating in the magical way we used to so long ago.

SANANDA speaks:

There is much misunderstanding about the nature of the antichrist energy. The antichrist is not one person. There are many beings who are carrying the antichrist energy. They are powerful beings who control your planet. Some are known to you and some are not. The ones who are known do not look or feel evil to you. They usually feel very magnetic, very charismatic. You feel drawn to them.

The antichrist energy is very seductive and many ways have been created to make you vulnerable to it. Much of your music has been negatively charged in a way that makes you susceptible to the antichrist energy. And this isn't just being done to rock and roll and rap music, much of the new age music that you are drawn to is also charged with this negative pulse. You must be able to feel what vibration is coming through the music you listen to. You must learn to feel deeply into the music to discern if it is positively or negatively charged.

There are beings on your planet who are channeling negative entities and saying they are channeling Light Beings. Those who do not have the discernment to know the difference are allowing these energies to come into them and create distortions in their energy fields that make them susceptible to the dark forces.

There are also incidences of very beautiful, spiritual, gifted teachers and healers who have been tricked into giving up their bodies to dark force energies. There is so much happening that you need to be aware of. We cannot say, "Don't go here. Don't listen to this. Don't look at that. Don't read that." All we can say is, "Hone your discernment so you know what energies you are receiving."

There are more successful people who are carrying antichrist energy than there are who are carrying Cosmic Christ Energy. Those carrying antichrist energy are not always the ones practicing black magic and witchcraft. Some are, but they are easy to identify. The ones who are the most dangerous are the ones who are saying the right words, who are in the right places, but yet are not delivering the right vibration.

This is a hard pill to swallow and very discouraging for the Light Beings who are trying so hard to reach people. The antichrist energy wraps around people and vibrates a frequency that is very chaotic. It will create separation between beings who truly belong together, all of the sudden there is no harmony. It will create energy rifts between people who had solidly-built relationships for long periods of time. You need to be aware of what's happening on your Earth plane, for the antichrist energy is controlling many people and continually seeks to find new ways to wrap around others. It is a very serious problem.

I am asking you to join me in my campaign to wake up others, to help them connect back up to the God Source and to show them how to protect themselves. This is very important. Those that you help will be so grateful and we, in Spirit, will be grateful also. There is much shifting of consciousness that needs to happen and when you shift your consciousness you open the way for others to shift theirs.

We are bringing in as much Light energy as possible to help you. I am asking you again to open and receive as much God Essence as you can take into your physical body, be the co-creator that you were meant to be, and direct this energy in the ways that will be most useful to you and others. Ask for all the help you need at every level and know there is an unlimited amount available to you. You can be as selfish as you want. God's Energy is available for you to take and use.

We can assist you in breaking up old energy patterns that are holding you stuck. We can assist you in building strong energy vortexes for your protection. Remember we are near and call on us often. Know we are always here, but you must ask or we cannot help you. You must ask and then be open to receive.

AFFIRMATIONS

I willingly release my blinders, the energetic patterns that hold me from truly seeing with my physical eyes what is truly going on around me.

I release all the distortions which interfere and keep my positive thoughts and visions from manifesting. Once they are removed the new ways of living that I visualize will manifest in my life.

I confidently seek out association with those who are strongly aligned with God's Light.

I am willing to flow with the great Earth changes. I have a positive attitude because I understand that as the Earth Mother releases her old form she will also be released from her suffering,
and so will I.

I am willing to support Mother Earth through her birthing process. As the Earth Mother releases her old form energy and births her new energetic pattern, I will also shed my old restrictive patterns.

I ask Spirit for help to break up all the old energy patterns that are holding me stuck. I ask for assistance to build strong energy vortexes of positive vibrations to protect myself and my loved ones.

QUESTIONS AND ANSWERS

ADRIENE:

Tonight I will channel from the group consciousness of the Ancient Hierarchy which consists of the Mother and Father aspects of God, Archangel Michael, Ashtar, Sananda and Mother Mary. They all will be present and I will attune to their group consciousness to answer your questions.

Q. We learned the other night that there could be negative influences in different musical formats. Could you expand on this information?

A. There are circuitries in the subtle body that are interfered with when certain vibrations hit them. This causes energies to be thrown off their right paths and creates imbalance and disharmony within all the bodies: spiritual, mental, emotional and vital. Think about having a very intricate circuit board within you that makes everything work. When negative vibrations hit this board they interfere with the way energies flow and create breaks in your circuitry. Openings are created that allow dark force energies to enter.

It is difficult to know when this is happening. One solution is to protect yourself with powerful positive vibrations that can override the negative pulses that you are constantly being bombarded with. More positively charged music is needed. It takes powerful doses of energy to override all of the wrong circuitry within, so you can feel Truth.

Q. The other night you talked about the serious earthquakes. Would it be beneficial to store large amounts of canned goods? If so, where would be the best location to store them?

A. It is very important that you consider fresh food and water sources. By fresh we mean food that has not been contaminated. So much of the foods that you eat are contaminated. You should be very diligent in clearing and purifying everything that you put into your mouth because almost everything has distorted energies in it at this time. It is important to have a confident attitude about survival. Developing your spiritual skills will give you more security than how much food you have stored in your cupboard.

Yet always use your common sense, for it will be important to have a stored supply of food and water for the periods when fresh food and water sources are not available. Also start to seek out others who you know will have access to food. Not everyone will grow and store food. It is time to start working cooperatively with each other. Your food and water should be stored in areas that are safe from negative vibrations. There are energy fields that are bombarding the Earth at this time which are keeping people in a frequency of panic, anxiety and depression.

Q. In the Saint Croix Valley, Wisconsin, there are rocks exposed from the original core of the Earth, wouldn't those rocks deflect any negative vibrations?

A. No, there is no safety in that. You must understand that the headquarters for the dark forces on Earth are inside the Earth. This is a well known fact. People have seen spacecraft going right into the Earth. There are very atrocious things going on inside the Earth. Your Earth has literally been gutted out.

To deflect negative vibrations you must maintain positive energy fields. That is why, again, we are suggesting that you join with other spiritually strong beings and form communities. Together you will be able to protect a large area. One fallacy is that there are protected places on Earth. You must take responsibility and protect areas.

If you have a community of four or five people and you are connecting up in consciousness with other communities of larger or smaller numbers, you are going to create a powerful gridwork that helps hold everyone's place safe. And while you are helping each other we will be able to assist because you have provided the necessary physical vehicles.

There are what we call inverted vortexes under all your major cities that pull your energies down into the underground cities of the dark forces. Many of you are feeling very ill and low in energy because no matter how much energy you bring through from Spirit, it gets pulled from you. Many spiritual healers and teachers are feeling so drained that they are choosing to leave their bodies.

We have developed ways to protect you. We have created Earth Chakra Protections that, when placed in your Earth chakras, do not allow this to happen. For every problem we have a solution. Until this time the solutions have not been known to the many. Oftentimes until something is fully developed it is kept very hidden, for with attention comes interference. It is time to make the solutions available to assist those who are committed to staying on Earth during the great changes.

We are asking you to be peaceful warriors. Work cooperatively with Spirit to hold energy fields that will protect you and your loved ones and help the Earth.

Q. Is it true that we are being bombarded with negative frequencies through our TV's, radios, telephones and electricity?

A. What you speak of is happening and most people would rather not hear your Truth because it is so uncomfortable to them. You should be careful about what you say on the telephone. Definitely be aware of what comes through your television. Less and less television watching is advised because the broadcasted frequencies truly are having an adverse affect on you. People who are aware notice that they get irritable if the TV is on for too long. The frequencies irritate your nervous systems and stress your immune systems.

Disruptive frequencies are coming through all of your electrical outlets. You must learn to clear the negative energy fields these frequencies create and seek out the technologies that will protect against this interference. It is a trying time you live in, we know it seems like an overwhelming task to overcome all of the obstacles that are preventing you from staying healthy and balanced. Don't give up. Each person must take some responsibility for what has been created and actively participate to instigate positive changes.

There will be much looting in the near future. You can learn to shield your personal property with energy fields. Those who are creating chaotic energy will be attracted to chaotic energy, this is what happens. There will be much looting of food, for many people will go back to gardening. You need to be aware of this potential problem.

We are not suggesting you run away and hide. We are asking you to be strong examples of balance. It will be difficult to maintain a strong balanced state unless you are being emotionally supported by others, this is yet another reason to form communities. Many communities are being guided to create vortexes which will allow us to come and be with you. This will be of the greatest help to you. We know how difficult it is for you to trust your own intuition because of the constant bombardment of interfering energies.

Your governments are monitoring all spacecraft that come and go from your planet. People who are sighting UFO's are mainly seeing the spacecraft of the extraterrestrials that are working with your governments. We are very careful not to get caught up in their interactions. We communicate with you, but we are not close, we are far away. We have a space station that we communicate from, a communication center. We will not be seen until the grand finale. At this time not enough people are in place to help us with this finale. There are areas in the Earth that have been protectively sealed which now need to be opened so we have entrance.

Q. It sounds like the immanent Earth changes will be very destructive.

Will we be living with electricity and gas powered cars and running water? What should we expect?

A. We do not want to frighten you into running out to buy horses! There will be a period of transition that will be uncomfortable on your planet. And yet, as you network you will find others who know alternatives to your traditional modes of transportation and electricity. These are the people you need to draw to you at this time. If you create enough Light in your community you will attract those to you who have all the necessary pieces.

Solar power will be extremely useful and it is now time to have your generators handy. Things will happen in progression. Think about what it would be like not to have running water. There will be sources of water available at all times. Some Lightworkers hold the technologies to purify and revivify stagnant water.

There is so much technology already on your planet that is not being allowed to come forward and that is why it is time to organize. So many of the Lightworkers holding knowledge have had to stay hidden to ensure their survival. There will be those who hoard gasoline and will be using automobiles for transportation.

Communication through satellites and other advanced technologies will be prevalent. We promise we will be sending evolved Light Beings with advanced technologies to Earth to help you. Once the way has been made and the negativity has been cleared, they will come and do their pieces. They will find you from the vibration that you are sending out and bring you their contribution.

You really need to be aware of what is resonating within you. Are you vibrating fear and panic, or are you vibrating your contribution? Even now there are organizations and companies that have much to offer you. Seek out these groups because they will survive the Earth changes and will be able to supply and distribute basic necessities. They are preparing. There is more going on than you realize and much has been kept at a grass root level so as not to draw too much attention from the powers that want to control.

There is going to be chaos and panic everywhere and that is why it is so important, again, that you are with a group that can hold peaceful energy. All of your major cities will be chaotic and under strict police control.

We want to make you aware that certain substances are being added to your food sources and have not been listed on the labels. Your governments have developed very underhanded ways of controlling people through substances. The drug companies are deeply involved with this conspiracy to keep people controllable like robots. Many drugs are being fed to people like candy.

These controlling substances are not only in the drugs you take, they are also used in the processing of coffee beans. Many additives are going into your coffee, tea, tobacco, and sugar-based products. We are not saying that every brand of coffee, tea, cigarettes, and candy have these controlling substances added, but many do. These substances are keeping you placated.

It is very difficult to know which brands are safe. It is better to just eliminate

183

these categories of items from your diet and lifestyle. Placation is being used to give you a false sense of security and keep you from being outraged at what is really going on.

Q. Would you expand on why the governments are putting these additives in items that are commonly consumed or used on a daily basis?

A. If you could feel what is truly going on you would be outraged and rally and organize with others to change things. When placated, you go along with what you are being programmed and fed. It is easy to control people who are placated. People who feel strongly about something will passionately work to create change. Your Earth is getting ready to wake everyone out of their slumber.

Q. Is the government aware of the coming Earth changes?

A. The government is very much aware of the coming Earth changes and is even plotting to benefit from them. There are complex scenarios being planned for power plays. God now wants His messengers to come forward and speak Truth and work cooperatively with the Earth changes. The government also has been grooming messengers and are now finding ways to deliver to the public what they want them to believe and do.

God's messengers are working cooperatively with Mother Earth to wake people up and make them aware so they will finally start to take personal responsibility for their own welfare. The government wants to stay in control.

They have several people already out in the public's eye who have very charismatic, magnetic energy that people are responding to. Large groups are gathering around them and following their teachings and messages.

This is a most dangerous situation. The Lightworkers on planet Earth are still not organized, many have even fallen into the illusion that there really is nothing for them to do, that we, the Hierarchy will rescue them. We cannot rescue anyone, including your Earth, without your participation!

There is literally a race going on between those carrying the antichrist energy and those carrying the Cosmic Christ Energy. The Cosmic Christ Energy is trying to wake people up and protect them. The antichrist energy wraps around people in an effort to control them and take over their soul essence.

One of the hardest realities for you to accept is the cloning of beings that is happening from your stolen soul essence. Clones have to be created from something, life is not created without essence.

Q. How was the antichrist created?

A. First of all, understand the antichrist is an energy, it is not one being. There are several very evil beings on your planet who are "implanted" beings, which means they were brought into physical form by the dark forces to carry this energy. The antichrist energy has been on your Earth plane since the beginning of dark force energy, but it has not always been as powerful as it is at this time. Many who hunger for power draw on this energy. Lucifer originally created this energy by stealing essence from Light Beings and converting it into a form of essence that serves his purpose. It is a form of energy, it is not a formed being, and yet this energy is carried by many different types of beings.

When the antichrist energy finds an opening in a person it infiltrates and subtly changes and manipulates their essence. Most often the person is not aware of being manipulated. It is a very serious situation. What often happens is the soul of the person gets so frightened when this is going on that it leaves and then another soul is brought in. This is usually a soul that has had a long-time association with dark force energies and will be easy to control and manipulate. This has happened with quite a few of your spiritual leaders, their souls became frightened when they felt their energy becoming manipulated and they left and allowed their bodies to be overtaken.

Q.   When is the Big Event most likely to occur?

A.   It is not a single event. When your world feels the most hopeless and heavy with suppression and depression, the great changes are near. You are now coming through the dark tunnel, you cannot yet see the Light because you are still in the dark tunnel. Soon you will see some shifting occurring in a positive direction. This is only going to create more resistance from those in power who have a strong hold at this time. What is needed is for the Light-workers to join forces and create a giant whip to break through the set old form energies. We are increasing the frequency of the energy that is being sent to you to push you in the right directions, and we encourage you to move quickly so we can activate God's Plan.

The antichrist energy works to keep people separate by playing on their lower natures to keep them from uniting. Did you ever try to get three people to agree on anything? We are not asking you to compromise your ideals, we are only suggesting that you stay focused on your goals and let go of some of the petty annoyances that are preventing successful team efforts. Processing your petty annoyances with each other is consuming valuable time!

You will appreciate each other's unique character when your survival depends on the group effort. Some of the people who have the most annoying traits to you will prove to be the greatest sources of comfort and help. And some of those you now count on and enjoy will fall apart and be of absolutely no help. So let go of a lot of your judgments about those around you.

Q. Could you name some places in the USA that might be more desirable to live in than others?

A. We are asking you to be where you are needed rather than where you think it is safe. You are all aware of the dangerous Earth conditions on the west coast, yet many people migrating east will be shocked to find unstable conditions wherever they go.

You would be wise to stay away from large areas of water. Major sources of water will be so disrupted causing a lot of flooding inland. Yet, there are ways to be assured of safety. You must become sensitive to the vibration of the land. We have been encouraging you to really start attuning to the Earth. When things are getting serious in your area it may mean a temporary move. Even in some of your communities you may need to move to safer ground for awhile and then come back.

You are going to be tested like you have never been tested before, and yet if you hold yourself in strong alignment with God, you will be fine. There is no real safety in any place unless you are holding a protective energy field. Land that people are predicting to be safe will be cluttered with destructive, chaotic people. People will be migrating out of cities and will eventually reach all of the rural areas. If you try to hide yourself up on a mountain, God may decide to open that mountain.

There are certain areas of your world that will be more devastated than others. Understand that as land masses are lost new land masses will surface, but they may not be able to support human habitation for a long time. It is going to be quite a project for the volunteers that stay and "ride the wave" as we are calling it in Spirit. You will experience a wave of progressive Earth changes.

There is no way to stop these changes, once they start they will continue, each one triggering the next one. The Earth must release and her crust will erupt. We want to see this release happen with the least amount of damage, like an unwinding. In some of your therapeutic processes you talk about unwinding old destructive patterns which are holding you stuck. That is exactly how we would like to see the Earth release. We do not want it to be one massive explosion. It can be a rather exciting process as well. Make sure you have a deck of cards for those long nights without television!

Q. You mentioned that during the devastation some people are going to be lifted up or evacuated?

A. There will be a lot of last minute hurry for those who are desiring to leave in this way. Those of you who know your role is to be evacuated with your physical bodies will all of a sudden get a tremendous impulse to be somewhere at the right time. There will not be much advance notice for these pick-ups. You will need to be at your designated pick-up place at exactly the right time, for we will not be able to wait for you. We will send you strong inner messages, "Now. Go now." We advise you to begin watching where your thoughts go, where does it feel like you need to be? You will be guided to an open portal where we can come through. Many portal entry points are not yet open. As the Earth releases we will be able to safely open more portals.

Q. Is our weather being manipulated?

A. Your weather patterns are being manipulated to achieve the results wanted by those who are controlling the conspiracies. This is something that will continue and will become more and more disruptive, and yet you have all forgotten that you have the ability to affect weather as well. With group consciousness you can create a current of energy in the atmosphere to disrupt this manipulation and regulate the weather patterns. We will help you. Send out the right vibrations to the atmosphere and we will join those vibrations from our end to achieve the desired results.

Do not accept any conditions you do not like, you can change them. But it will take a group effort because a lot of energy is needed to shift an entire weather pattern. You must pay attention and begin to participate. You should also be experimenting with the technologies to grow food in artificial environments that are not dependent on external conditions.

We will always help you work with what you have. There are many technologies for growing food quickly and under adverse conditions. These are already being experimented with by several groups of people. Others are working on ways to potentize food so it will hold vital energy while being stored. We will help you build environmentally controlled cities on Earth, after the great changes, in areas that will not support human life.

There are cities inside the Earth that have been created by beings who are not of God Essence. When the Earth begins to shake many people will be drawn to these underground cities thinking they will be safe and taken care of. We are warning you strongly, this is not where you want to be, for you will be completely controlled. All of your freedoms will be taken away. Your governments will be sending strong messages stating these underground cities have been created for your welfare and safety. Please be strong and stay on the Earth's surface where we can help you.

We will show you ways to build adequate shelters, grow food and purify your air and water. It is going to be challenging and yet it can be done, think of what can be done with only a simple greenhouse. You need to start looking at this more and more. Also learn about potentizing. There are ways to potentize foods so you can eat less and get more from what you take in. You constantly consume quantities of unnecessary food. Your bodies will function properly when given the right amount of nutrients, and this can be done with very little food. Do not be afraid to give up your comfort eating. You will not be eating meat and potatoes. And those who suggest that you stock up with livestock and chickens are not being realistic. You will not have the food stuffs to feed them.

You must think futuristic. Activate the information you are carrying within, bring it forward and make it available to those who are seeking. There are people who will respond and sponsor your projects with large sums of money. They are waiting for you to come forward so they can fulfill their missions as well. You're not in this alone. You came in with a group who have been aligned with different components to the same project. We are not unfamiliar with the workings of your world. We know monetary means are needed, and those people who are to support your projects are waiting. This all needs to happen very, very quickly.

Q. What about mortgages and things like that? If all of our systems break down, what will happen to our employment?

A. There is going to be a complete breakdown of systems, but understand that this is necessary for a fresh start. Industry and employment, as you know it, will not exist. Think about the master computer having the plug pulled. Life will not be as you know it. Money will not matter. You must be able to take care of yourselves for a short period of time until we can reach you and support you.

We have been encouraging you to become involved in cottage industries and services which provide something that people will always need. Your corporate world of paper pushing will no longer exist. We are not suggesting that all of you in the corporate world immediately quit your jobs, many of you are adding helpful energies to your workplaces and this is important also.

It is extremely important that you tune in and see what changes you need to make to be in the right place at the right time to take advantage of the right situations. Your current systems will no longer exist. Your governments are preparing for this. They have already created their plans. They have camps ready to corral people who are out of control and cannot provide for their own basic needs. One of the worst scenarios we anticipate is people just running scared, rather than staying put and dealing with what is going on around them, and that is what will create the real chaos. There will always be those who have supplies and will be willing to sell their goods. You will need something of equal value to barter with. Money is only functional in your current system.

Worrying about saving up enough money for your retirement is a waste of your energy. Your money is needed now for projects to put things in place. It is time to use your money to create safe, self-sufficient communities and systems to communicate and share resources with others. How are you planning to help those who have nothing? Those of you who have resources have a responsibility to use those resources to make a difference now. Your life insurance, stocks and bonds will have no value. Create money now and use it to secure your futures. Instead of worrying about how to get dental insurance, you should be looking for a dentist to join your community. Try to have a jack-of-all-trades in your community.

Q. How can we help the people out on the west coast, like friends and family who are not open to this kind of information?

A. There is absolutely nothing you can do but accept that they are making their decisions and choices. Please understand that many people are willing to leave your planet now. They do not want to stay through the great Earth changes. They are putting themselves exactly where they want to be to leave the Earth plane. The best thing to do is connect with their High Selves and help them make their transition. They can always get another body, but their souls will need help finding their way through the astral planes. The dark forces have set many traps to capture souls. Dying is no longer an easy process of just going into the Light. Many will die with confusion and fear which increases their risk of getting trapped.

You can share knowledge, but how it is received is not something you can control. Everyone living in California is aware of the risk, and yet people are still choosing to be there. One of the hardest things you will have to deal with will be the loss of loved ones.

Q. You mentioned that plague energy is widespread. Can you tell us where it comes from, what type of organism it is and what we can do about this problem?

A. First of all you are not going to get anywhere with identifying organisms because it is an energy field that attracts all kinds of illnesses to it. Many mutations and different strains of known illnesses will be activating in people's systems. The solutions to this problem are to clear all energies and belief systems within you that resonate to the low frequencies of diseases and illnesses, keep emotionally balanced and strive to bring in and hold powerful God Vibrations to which nothing negative can attach.

Q. Are our governments creating this plague energy?

A. Yes. Your governments are being used by the dark powers. Your governments think that they have some kind of control, when actually they are being used by the master conspirators who are promising them all kinds of power, and yet will eliminate them when they are no longer useful. This is what usually happens to people who align with dark energy. Whatever power is gained is taken from them.

Q. Are the plagues the result of karma?

A.   No. These conditions are not karmic in nature. Much of what is happening on your planet is due to outside influences and that is why God is intervening. Universal Law is not being respected.

Many of you are still functioning within old belief systems concerning karma. You hold a lot of karmic situations in your energy fields that you could easily release and be free of instead of creating a lot of painful experiences. You need to learn and grow and evolve, yet you do not need to punish yourselves for your mistakes. Learn your lessons and move along. Quit holding yourself in painful situations.

Q.   About how many people/souls will decide to leave of their own Free Will or will just die during the Earth changes? What percentage of the population will leave?

A.   The loss of population will be very high, right now it is as high as three-fourths that will leave. We are still hoping that more will stay to help with the changes, but right now there is little hope of more than one-fourth being alive.

Q.   Are we going to experience a geocentric pole shift?

A.   Yes, the pole shift will definitely occur. Even though it will cause devastation, it will also eliminate a lot of problems. The Earth truly needs to shift in this way.

Q.   Are you saying that even during the extreme devastation there is a reason for us to stay on the Earth?

A.   There is definitely a reason to stay.   Your help is needed for the rebuilding, but also to help ground the energies necessary to ensure the Earth's successful transition.   We need volunteers to stay and hold these energies throughout the changes.   We want all of you who are willing to stay to be comfortable and supported.   Remember that the Earth changes will release the tremendous compacted stuck energy and allow God's Magical Energy to assist those of you who have weathered the storm.

An extreme amount of clean-up will be needed and we will help you with that.   The doors will be wide open for all of our confederations to bring you the technologies for the rebuilding.   We will not abandon you.   We will work cooperatively as brothers and sisters.   Some of you will join us on our Light vehicles and learn from us and then return to your planet to share your knowledge with others.

Q.   In the final end, will Lucifer's dark energy be lifted as well?

A.   It will no longer be possible for Lucifer's dark energy to have a hold on Earth once the vibrations do not support it.   The Earth, and all of those who can move with her, will be pulled out of range of Lucifer's reach.   Your Earth Mother will at last be freed from her bondage and allowed to flow with the higher energies, taking her rightful place in God's Creation.

Epilogue

I began searching for Truth when I was a young child. The world around me seemed so empty, meaningless and unfulfilling that I felt certain a loving God of goodness wouldn't have created it this way. Why was He allowing it? What had gone wrong and how could it be corrected? What was the meaning of life anyway? I had so many demanding questions and the answers seemed nowhere to be found. At times I got sidetracked, but my restless inner prompting, as well as my life circumstances didn't allow me to put aside my search for too long.

My quest lead me to study most major religions, philosophies and beliefs. I survived a major car accident which left me widowed and in great physical and emotional pain. The medical profession did what they could and then told me I must live with constant pain. I turned to alternative forms of healing and energy therapies in my search for physical healing. I studied the mind and worked with hypnosis to reprogram my mental body. Everything I tried offered some truths and relief, yet still left me feeling dissatisfied. I knew something was missing because the deep questions remained unresolved and the happiness and inner peace I sought still eluded me.

One day I observed a friend take an incredible leap after a healing session with Adriene Wentworth. I immediately contacted Adriene. This lead to my first-hand experience of the power and dramatic results obtained with the Christa Healing method. I have now taken more leaps, in my healing and spiritual processes, than I ever dreamed possible in one lifetime. My restored physical health and vitality, along with my strong inner connection to Spirit testify to the power of Adriene's work and knowledge. With my strong Christa Protection in place, my psychic and intuitive abilities are strong, powerful and accurate. I now confidently trust and rely on my own inner guidance and connection to God.

Adriene's clear and deep understanding of the spiritual process lead her to uncover the keys to what is interfering and preventing us from reconnecting to the Source and feeling His Energy and presence in our lives in a real way. Knowledge of the conspiracies that Adriene has uncovered and explained in her book, Divine Intervention, has helped me understand, at last, how we lost our alignment with God's Light, how we were tricked into giving up our power and energy, and what interferes with our ability to see this clearly and take action. The deep questions that haunted me for so long have now been resolved and the solutions are clearly understood.

The focus of Adriene's work is to help all God's children get back in their personal power and reconnect up to the Source. To do this we must first disconnect from the negative energies and remove their interferences from our energy bodies. My life has been filled with a deep sense of meaning and empowerment as I move forward on my journey free of these impediments. I now understand fully my role as co-creator and my personal responsibility to do my part along with God, rather than blaming Him for everything that happens in my life, or thinking it's all up to me.

During her spiritual process, and through much self-sacrifice and dedicated hard work, Adriene reached and brought through the Christa Energy to this plane. This Energy is here at this time to assist mankind and is available to all who desire it. The Christa Protection is God's solution to the intense interference we encounter on Earth at this time. It allows us to continue to evolve free of the entanglement and influence of these distorted energies. I have carried the Christa Energy for a number of years and it has transformed my being and life. The Christa Energy is powerful and strong, yet incredibly loving and gentle. Bringing this Energy in through my physical vehicle has greatly facilitated my personal healing process.

Epilogue

After I had the brain-stem implant and other interferences removed, my spiritual growth and level of consciousness have expanded beyond my greatest hopes. This process also helped me get in touch with my soul's mission. My self confidence, inner happiness, peace, and sense of purpose and connectedness are a source of stability, contentment and joy despite my changing outer-life circumstances.

My heart overflows with deep love, admiration and gratitude to Adriene for her perseverance, determination and dedication to Truth which lead her to uncover these atrocious conspiracies and to painstakingly find the necessary solutions. As each interference is uncovered Adriene works hand-in-hand with Spirit to develop the techniques to release the problem and restore health and balance. My life has been blessed immeasurably because of my association with her.

Adriene's strong allegiance and devotion to Christ, along with her deep love for mankind and all children everywhere, has helped her find the courage to come forward publicly and expose these conspiracies and help all God's children realign with their wholeness.

Tara Lakshmi Tindall
Louisville Colorado
May 1997

THE CHRISTA HEALING

Christa Healing is a unique and powerful method of healing developed by Adriene Wentworth after many years of study and private practice in the field of alternative health care. For complete healing, it is important to release all of the blockages in the physical, emotional, mental and spiritual energy bodies that are preventing you from successfully shifting to a state of health and well-being. The Christa Healing method identifies your patterns of imbalance and releases them at the core level causing vibrational changes that work through each of the bodies and result in physical cellular change enhancing the body/mind's ability to self-heal.

The Christa Healing can effectively remove unknown influences that have been affecting you negatively and holding you powerless to move forward in your spiritual development and healing process, such as:

- Cordings and other people's energies
- E.T. abductions and interference
- Implants, devices and distorted energies
- Entities and dark force influences
- Impressions from traumatic past and present life experiences
- Imprints from unwanted behavior patterns
- Limiting belief systems
- Denied parts of self that work against the healing process

The Christa Healing gives you choice to move past:

- Acute and chronic illnesses
- Depression, fear and phobias
- Dysfunctional and unfulfilling relationships
- Sexual, emotional, mental or physical abuses
- Adverse behavior patterns and addictions
- Unwanted attachments and limitations
- Dark force conspiracies that hold you stuck
- Physical, emotional, mental and spiritual blocks

Much can be cleared away in one session and clarity is given to the original cause of your problems, empowering and activating you to create wholeness, wellness and balance in your body, mind and spirit. The Christa Healing method can help you wake up your gifts and abilities and get in touch with your soul's mission.

If you are not able to be physically present for a healing session, practitioners can send a distant healing. Your session is recorded on audio tape and mailed to you.

LEVEL 1 CHRISTA ENERGY ATTUNEMENT

Adriene Wentworth has brought through a new healing energy called the "Christa Energy" which is Cosmic Christ Energy in a vibration with specific intent to awaken, protect, self-heal and manifest on the physical plane. The Christa Energy will help you awaken to new levels of awareness and potential. The Christa Energy is powerful enough to protect against the antichrist energy which is preying heavily on the Earth and her inhabitants.

When you are attuned to the Christa Energy your soul is protected from outside interferences and strong fields of protection are woven within your energy bodies allowing you to evolve to the highest frequency and not be affected by surrounding lower vibrations. The Christa protection does not allow negative energies to penetrate your energy bodies and yet will allow you to work with all energies that are aligned with God's Light. The Christa Energy complements and enhances all other healing energies. Carrying and using the Christa Energy enables you to hold all high vibrational energies and effectively ground them into the physical plane.

If you are dedicated to helping humanity and the Earth evolve and would like to accelerate your own spiritual development and healing process, you may be attuned to carry the Christa Energy. When you bring the Christa Energy into your bodies it pushes out all of your hidden blocks, resistances and denials. The Energy will give you strength and help you stay balanced and centered through the challenges of these changing times. It will help you get in touch with your purpose for being on Earth at this time and help support you to move forward with that purpose. Once you receive this Energy, it will spontaneously flow out of your heart and protect the souls of all who open to receive it.

The Earth needs to receive this Energy to complete her spiritual evolution and is asking for volunteers to help channel this Energy to her. No special skills or abilities are required to carry the Christa Energy, just sincerity of heart to use it in the way God intends.

LEVEL 2 CHRISTA ENERGY ATTUNEMENT

After you have worked with the Christa Energy for 90 days and your protection is complete, you can be attuned to the next level of the Energy which is coded for manifesting on the physical plane. The Christa Energy will assist you in creating what you need to move forward in your own spiritual growth and personal development. This Energy is here to help us become co-creators once again with God. For the Energy to be effective, your desires and intent must be in alignment with God and work for the highest good of all. This Energy cannot be abused in any way. Instructions and guidance will be given to assist you in developing your manifesting abilities.

Once you have mastered the creative level of the Christa Energy, you will automatically reach and bring through the third level of the Energy which is for the ascension process.

If you are not able to be physically present, you can be attuned to this Energy from a distance. Your attunement and instructions are recorded on audio tape and mailed to you.

LECTURES AND INSPIRATIONAL EVENTS

Adriene Wentworth is an experienced speaker who has traveled extensively promoting her healing ministry and demonstrating her transformative abilities. Adriene is a spokesperson for the Ancient Hierarchy and transmits their powerful spiritual energies. Adriene touches people with the direct experience of God's love and energy. Those who attend her events experience spontaneous healings and awakenings and greater levels of clarity and awareness. While speaking, Adriene transforms negative energies and balances inharmonious energy fields.

Adriene passionately delivers powerful, revealing, Truth messages to help people overcome their obstacles and find their way to the Real within and the Greater Source from which they came. Her messages inspire and give hope, yet are not colored or sugar-coated for comfort.

Adriene and her trained staff provide inspirational events, lectures, classes, individual healing sessions and Christa Energy Attunements throughout the world.

For more information, contact:

Christa Resources
P.O. Box 696
Prior Lake, MN 55372
(MN phone/fax: 612-403-0594)

Visit our website at: http://www.ChristaResources.com
e-mail: awentworth@ChristaResources.com

GARUDA FOUNDATION

The Garuda Foundation is a non-profit organization established by Adriene Wentworth in 1994 to help support her dream of assisting people to become co-creators with God and teach them how to achieve mastery over their own existence.

Garuda is a Sanskrit word meaning "Eagle of God." God provides for all of our needs and sends His blessings to us in many forms through His instruments. These instruments (eagles) hear the call, resonate with the cause and provide the means to accomplish the goals.

The Garuda Foundation supports many different charitable, spiritual, educational, scientific and humanitarian purposes. The primary objective of the Foundation is to provide the general public with the alternative healing modalities, educational programs and resource materials that will assist them with their spiritual development and personal growth. This growth will help them achieve wellness and balance at all levels: physical, emotional, mental and spiritual. The goals of the Garuda Foundation are to:

Inspire mankind to awaken and align with their spiritual natures;

Guide mankind through the awakening process and empower them to live their own truth and bring forward their soul's mission;

Provide healing modalities that will assist mankind in becoming healthy and whole at all levels of their being: physical, emotional, mental and spiritual;

Provide education and support for spiritual development and the healing process as mankind shifts in consciousness and releases old patterns to restructure their lives;

Teach universal truths and principles that enhance self-mastery and co-creating with God;

<u>Create self-sufficient communities</u> implementing new healthy systems in harmony with God and the forces of nature.

The tax-exempt 501(c)(3) status of the Garuda Foundation is gained through an account maintained with the National Heritage Foundation, Inc. National Heritage Foundation, Inc. is a pioneer in the donor-advised fund movement and provides the Garuda Foundation with administration and monitoring of its charitable funds. Through this unique organizational structure, it is possible to support the Garuda Foundation while enjoying all the tax benefits that accompany charitable contributions. Send all donations to:

NATIONAL HERITAGE FOUNDATION, INC.   GARUDA FOUNDATION
Box 1776   is a "charitable project of
6129 Leesburg Pike, Suite 1207   the National Heritage
Falls Church, VA 22041   Foundation, Inc."
(703) 820-2079

Please make checks payable to: <u>National Heritage Foundation, Inc.</u>
                                                             Federal Tax ID Number: 58-2085326

And include on the Memo: "<u>Garuda Foundation, Account #5189</u>"

Water in the Eyes of Time
by Adriene Wentworth

Mantras are pure vibrational sounds of God which can be empowered to bear fruit to all who repeat them with sincerity of heart and pure intent. Each sacred mantra has a seer who has heard the word of God. A mantra also has a meter which is in consonance with the creation of the Universe. Hidden within that mantra is the presiding deity over that vibration. Deities are different vibrational aspects of God. The main part of a mantra is the shakti or the power which reveals itself to the devotee who invokes that mantra.

The mantras on <u>Water in the Eyes of Time</u> are empowered mantras which are like living seeds that will assist you with your healing and protection. These mantras are holding the energy of all the great beings of Light who have experienced the superconscious states that the vibrations of the mantras represent. Most people only think of using mantras in meditation to achieve high spiritual states, yet, I have found that each mantra has hidden within different levels of power and intent.

During my own spiritual journey, I became aware of the need to clear and release energies that block and interfere with the healing and spiritual growth process. Mantras are a powerful force that I use daily in my healing practice. Their vibrations are protective for both the healer and the client. Mantras can effectively release attached entities, ghosts and dark force energies which are preying on everyone on the Earth plane at this time.

As the Earth and its inhabitants move through the transitioning out of 3rd dimensional energy toward the 5th dimensional energy, the astral planes of the 4th dimension have become very loose and many beings from this plane are infiltrating both the aware and the unaware. If you are working on your spiritual growth process and increasing your Light, you will draw many of these beings to you because your Light will be seen and many will come for help, and others will come to interfere. It is very important for everyone to know how to keep themselves, their children and loved ones clear and protected. It is for this reason that my Spiritual Guidance urged me to create <u>Water in the Eyes of Time</u>.

ABOUT THE AUTHOR

Adriene Wentworth is a spiritual healer, teacher and spokesperson for the Spiritual Hierarchy which is guiding humanity and the Earth through this period of change and evolution. She has traveled to India three times to study with Himalayan Masters. Adriene has been active in the fields of holistic health, healing and spirituality for the past fifteen years. After many years of study and private practice, Adriene developed the Christa Healing method, which is a unique and powerful form of healing that clears the energy bodies from known and unknown influences. She believes this clearing work is the missing key in most people's healing process. In 1993, Adriene brought through a new energy called the "Christa Energy" which is Cosmic Christ Energy in a vibration with specific intent to awaken, protect, self-heal and manifest on the physical plane.

In 1994 Adriene established the Garuda Foundation, a non-profit organization that is devoted to assisting people in becoming co-creators with God and teach them how to have mastery over their own existence. Adriene and her trained staff provide classes, lectures, individual healing sessions and Christa Energy Attunements in various locations throughout the world. Adriene also provides inspirational events with high level healing and powerful divine messages. Her mission is to touch people with the direct experience of God's Love and Energy.